FINDING
A BALANCED
CONNECTION

*Build well-being from within,
take back your life and permanently
change it for the better.*

John-Paul Davies

Revised and updated edition: November 2019

First published: March 2019

ISBN: 978-1-7075693-7-3

Edited by Julia Kellaway

Cover design: Mark Yates
www.pfmhouse.com

Typesetting: David Siddall Multimedia
www.davidsiddall.com

Illustrations: Dan Shufflebotham

www.thistrustedplace.co.uk

Contents

John-Paul Davies is an experienced and accredited psychotherapist and counsellor running busy private practices in both London and Surrey. He specialises in working with adults experiencing difficulties such as anxiety, stress management, depression, addictions and compulsions, co-dependence, lack of meaning and purpose, narcissism, issues around sex and sexuality, and lack of self-esteem and confidence. Prior to training as a therapist, John-Paul worked as a solicitor in large private practices in the City of London for over 10 years.

Distilling and integrating psychotherapeutic and psychological theories and neuroscience, as well as the lessons John-Paul learned in his own personal journey from stressed City solicitor to contented psychotherapist, this book is the result of years of working successfully with a wide range of clients. *Finding A Balanced Connection* isn't a psychotherapy book as such; it's what John-Paul wished he'd known decades ago and wants you to know now.

Acknowledgements

To my wife, Tracy, and daughter, Evie, for tirelessly showing me what love means and feels like.

To my wonderful friends and family –
thank you for everything.

To my clients past, present and future for your trust and courage. Working with you is genuinely an honour.

And to Prince, for your humanity and fearlessness, and all the inspiration.

Introduction

Never before have so many of us had our physical and practical needs met, and so much opportunity to meet our emotional needs. Of course, there's poverty, disease and war in the world, but if you're reading this book, you're likely to be physically safe, protected by laws and police forces, with access to healthcare and education. At no other point in time have we had such a breadth of support, knowledge and experience literally at our fingertips.

Yet, despite unprecedented actual levels of comfort, safety and protection, our contentment and satisfaction are just not following suit. Rates of anxiety and stress, addiction, depression, self-harm, suicide, narcissism, eating disorders, aggression, loneliness and complex psychiatric conditions seem to increase year on year. Why, when we could be nurturing ourselves and exploring a world of opportunities from a base of relative safety, are we instead depressed, anxious and addicted, and often lacking a sense of direction and purpose?

I have written this book in the hope of answering that question. Part 1 sets out in some detail what I see as the problem, how it might manifest and why. I appreciate this can all make pretty heavy reading at times and may also trigger some difficult feelings for you, but please do try to persevere, because Parts 2 and 3 are all about solutions and ways forward; about how, and why, life can get better for you – right now.

Working through the book you'll come to see that it's how you think, feel and, therefore, behave that cause a great amount of your distress and that you need to look inside yourself to find out why. I'll introduce 10 principles designed to give you some tools to create and navigate a more purposeful, fulfilled and enjoyable life. This practical guide will show you how to build well-being from within, take back your life and permanently change it for the better.

Part 1

Your Brain

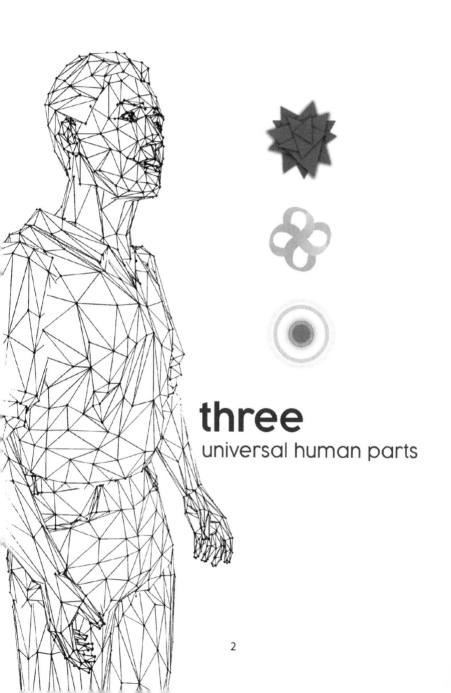

three
universal human parts

CHAPTER 1

Threat, Reward and Connection

You house the most powerful supercomputer ever known: your brain. Unfortunately, there's no user's manual for this complex machine. You're probably therefore often mismanaging it, sometimes to devastating effect in terms of your well-being.

Simplistically, your brain is made up of:

1. Threat
2. Reward
3. Connection

Respectively, these meet your basic human needs for safety, reward/satisfaction and connection.

Threat

Threat's purpose is to identify and respond quickly to aspects of your external environment that it perceives as endangering your physical and/or psychological safety. In terms of real threats to you, it's key to your survival. Acting as your panic room, threat fires up quick, protective health and safety messages and prompts immediate, automatic fight, flight or freeze behaviours to deal with the threat.

Threat is the part of the brain that makes you tense and scan the faces of the cabin crew when turbulence lasts longer than usual on a flight, or that prompts you to avoid walking down a dark alleyway at midnight in favour of the path with streetlights. In everyday life, it's also the part that lives for to-do lists, and worries about and identifies both actual and potential flaws and problems, prompting concerns such as: 'I need to be at that important appointment by 3pm. What do I have to be worried about that might mean I could miss it?' or 'That person seems a little cold towards me this week. I wonder why they don't like me.' In conversation, it includes all the 'he said, she said' stuff; the

fight/flight/freeze

embarrassment

anger

jealousy

guilt

survival

Threat

fear

regret

shame

disconnecting

protection

victim/perpetrator

complaints and the criticisms you might engage in with a friend over coffee or a glass of wine.

Threat was one of the first parts of the human brain to develop – it protected us from the mammoth outside the cave door – and, because its purpose is so important, we have a natural bias towards its red flags and alarms. It's always watching for, predicting and responding to problems, scanning for bad news, focusing on it and fast-tracking any 'threatening' experiences to our unconscious memory. It's interesting to note that we have no similar facility in our brain for good experiences, as we'll look at later. In the process of doing this, threat is always disconnecting us psychologically from our environment. Where this can save our physical and/or psychological life, I call this 'helpful threat'.

Because your survival might depend on it, threat necessarily makes simple and snap judgements. Based in the amygdala in your brain (the region associated with emotions), it has a 'negativity bias', meaning it **only** notices the bad, never registering either **an absence of bad, or the good**. So if you're worried you're too short, threat will only notice all the tall people at the party. If you're taking time to get pregnant, threat will notice all the pregnant women. Worried about how quickly you're progressing at work, threat focuses your attention only on the people being promoted. This bias constantly reminds you to forget how great you, others and the world you live in actually are.

Threat is made up of threat thoughts, threat feelings and threat behaviours:

Threat thoughts

Imagine you're watching Netflix and eating pizza in bed at 11pm. You hear the sound of the back door gently opening, followed by unidentified footsteps across the wooden floor of your living room. As hungry as you were before you heard the noise, the chances are you no longer want that pizza or are still enjoying *Stranger Things*. Instead, in a state of panic, perhaps having initially frozen for a few seconds, you leave the joys of food and TV, open the window and climb out onto the garage roof to escape and call the police.

Just as you're about to dial 999, you look back into the bedroom and see your partner walking sheepishly through the door, back early after an evening out and making poor decisions based on the amount of alcohol they have consumed. It wasn't, after all, a sociopathic burglar in your home, but the person you love most in the world. You shout at them and tell them never to do that again.

You can see from the above example that, when experiencing the world through threat, without question, you sacrifice potential sources of reward – in this case TV and pizza – based on a totally imagined problem. Your anger then also denies you the enjoyment of connection with your partner for some time after.

Looking at the characteristics of your threat thoughts in such moments, you can see you probably believe the following:

- The threat is coming for **you** (it's **personal**) and this situation won't go away on its own (it's **permanent**). You're narrowly focused on the **short-term**, **stuck** in a moment in time, **closed off** and letting go of all other thoughts of past, present and future for this perceived threat. What's happening is necessarily **pervasive and dominant; it's all you can see**. You're **solely focused** on it to the exclusion of all else. It's actually dangerous to divert your attention elsewhere.

- Without some kind of quick response you'll be injured or dead – you're **predicting** and **reaching forward** to the ultimate **catastrophic** scenario.

- You believe you'll **definitely** be harmed, rather than **possibly** harmed in these moments – you **make the possible probable**. You're predicting the intention of the 'threat' with certainty, without any communication with its source, suddenly a mind reader. You're in a state of being **certain about something (the operation of another's mind) that it's actually impossible to know**.

- If you were to stay where you are, your continued survival would depend entirely on the 'threat'. You're its potential **victim, trapped and blocked**. It's the 'threat' source that will allow you to live or not, and it's devoid of compassion and won't be reasoned with. It's all bad, inhuman, **a presumed sociopath**.

- This 'threatening situation' necessitates a largely automatic reaction, i.e. you're in a **reactive** state that eclipses proactive capacity for anything other than threat behaviours. You went out of the window **automatically, without question, or much conscious choice**.

- Importantly, your attention is **wholly outside of yourself**, except for your perception of self as **victim**. You are **entirely outward-in looking**, scanning the environment, filling in any blanks with your threat thoughts. When threat is too dominant, your **outward attention/hyper-vigilance to your external environment is always necessarily more important than inward attention**.

Threat behaviours

As mentioned above, threat has very limited, inflexible behaviours in its toolbox: just fight, flight and freeze (the last of which can also be characterised as physical and/or psychological collapse, dissociation or paralysis). You can see why: you might be dead if this were a real threat and you spent time consciously working through nuanced behavioural options.

Threat feelings

Threat feelings include those you'd expect to experience when facing something intent on harming you, i.e. fear, tension, nervousness, awkwardness, discomfort, stress, anger, rage, shock, hatred, revulsion and disgust. When threat gets triggered in relationships with others in life – when the threat is more psychological – your threat feelings are labelled as jealousy, guilt, regret, shame, embarrassment and envy, which we'll explore further below.

Threat in everyday relationships

You can see threat isn't your place of sophisticated reasoning, memory or perspective. What's 'true' for you when threat comes

short-termist

achieving goals

completing
missions/tasks

food

money

status

Reward

fun

sex

impulsive

temporary highs

entertainment

winning

forward depends on what your amygdala tells you is the biggest problem in the moment. Now imagine your amygdala is triggered most of the time, when you're dictated by threat. Just look again at the emboldened words on pages 6 and 7 and think about the cumulative effect they'd have on your perception of yourself and others in everyday relationships, and your likely behaviour. It's clear that threat would now be leading to lots of unhelpful disconnection, by unintentionally being used in the wrong places.

Let's say your boss doesn't smile at you this morning because she found out her partner is having an affair and is understandably disconnected. Your threat thoughts conclude that she frowns because she doesn't like you (**personal and being certain about something it's actually impossible to know** in these circumstances), that she'll never like you (**permanent, pervasive and narrowly focused on the moment**), because she's hard-faced with no capacity for empathy (**dehumanised, presumed sociopath**), but also because no one actually really likes you because you're not a likeable person (**pervasive and victim position**), that you'll eventually get found out that you can't do this job at all and get fired, in fact they're all probably planning it now... etc. (**'imposter syndrome', reach forward to predicted catastrophe, victim**).

This predictably leads to threat feelings. The threat thoughts and threat feelings bounce off each other, resulting in threat behaviours that, in turn, can actually cause a **real** problem. Threat behaviour choices are limited to: avoiding your boss (flight), being hostile the next time you have the opportunity, or more likely behind her back, and/or passive aggressively expressing anger towards her for the imagined slight (fight); or clamming up when she's around (freeze). These behaviours all confuse and annoy your upset boss. Threat has turned an imagined problem into a potentially real one – its self-fulfilling prophecy.

Although threat always believes it's protecting you, unless someone is coming at you with a knife and therefore you need helpful threat's reactive deployment of quick and dirty behaviours, threat is usually unhelpful when left in charge. It isn't a useful place from which to navigate your complicated life because it only knows how to identify and create problems, lacking empathy for others. When your brain uses threat too much, it will find a problem in whatever happens: if you get a new job, it's, 'Oh no, I got the job, I'm not going to be able to do it because I'm not good enough'; if you didn't get the job, it's, 'Oh no, I didn't get the job because I'm not good enough.' And it's the same if you're looking at someone else: if they don't clean up, they're annoying; if they do clean up, they're annoying because they didn't do it like you would have done. Threat damns us all if we do and damns us all if we don't.

In summary, to factor in potential problems when planning your journey to that meeting to make sure you're not late is helpful threat, but to imagine that when you're in the meeting a colleague you're not keen on is going to maul you in front of people is not – that's crossed the invisible line in your imagination into unhelpful threat. In order to lead a happier, more purposeful, more balanced life, you need to know the difference between these two, and know where this invisible line should be drawn in your mind.

Reward

Reward contains your innate, rewarded drives and motivations: to eat, have sex, achieve goals/complete missions/tasks and to win and compete with others, particularly for resources (more stuff, more status, more money). You can see why these behaviours are rewarded from an evolutionary point of view: they initiated and have since sustained human existence and can provide healthy motivational energy for us to act. To the extent that these drives can give you pleasure/fun/entertainment and motivate you to move forward personally and professionally as part of a balanced life, I call them 'helpful reward'.

However, as you may know, reward has the capacity to be hijacked by all kinds of behaviours and substances (including the food, sex, winning and getting more stuff it's designed to encourage), **to become the primary relationship in life, often at the expense of connection and even safety**. Once it's hijacked, you might find yourself compelled to continue chasing reward, despite problems, to lessen the mood dip set up by engaging it the last time (see page 40). Problems arise when reward has grown to dominate your life at the expense of your relationship with self and others.

Reward thoughts have a number of similarities to threat thoughts, such as always looking for the present moment to be different, their short-termism and intrusiveness and their focus on the wave and not the sea of life. What you need to hold in mind is that, for reward, other than an initial moment of satisfaction, of achieving the goal, whatever the behaviour or substance is, however much you have, **it'll never be enough**. The high of reward always ends eventually – think of it in terms of forever trying to fill up a cup with no bottom. You'll never eat enough cake, complete enough tasks, have sex with enough people, pop enough corks or earn enough money to permanently satisfy it. Reward will grasp, strive, cling and continually point you to a **lack of**. You may just be too heavily investing in something that has a very limited pay-off compared to connection. As you may know though, it isn't easy to let go of something that **almost works every time**.

By engaging in the rewarding behaviour, you may even think you're 'getting it out of your system', but actually you're getting it in, potentially forming a situation where reward controls you, rather than the other way around. I've often heard from people having lots of sexual contact with different partners that they're getting it out of their system so they can settle down comfortably with one person at some point in the future. I think it's actually the other way around – they're conditioning their brain to need more and more of this behaviour, which can be a really hard habit to break.

Annexed to this is when reward drives you to try to be better than and have more than others, living in a constant state of striving, comparison and competition – I call this 'status reward'. Living in a perpetual state of seeking reward, provides highs which are at best fleeting and, at worst, develop into the addictions/compulsions that can be so damaging to your long-term well-being. By doing the latter they compound threat, as you bounce between threat and reward in, at its most extreme, a 'feeding or fleeing', or, more crudely, 'fucking or fighting' life. Reward needs a lid on it to curb the delusional, compulsive, constant craving, unlimited excesses of its impulses and desires.

inspiration

grief

contentment

compassion

gratitude

peace

friendship

connection

love

growth

acceptance

freedom

empathy

trust

attunement

Connection

From the perspective of threat, connection might be sweet-talking, sentimental, cheesy, mushy, 'gone soft', even weak. But it's the part you feel happiest and most content in. Whereas existing mostly in threat means living defensively, **a life in connection means living on purpose**. Connection is your place of care for self and others, affection, friendship, soul mates, meaning and purpose, attunement, healing, creativity, opportunity, space, calm, loyalty, commitments, unity, empathy, honour, fond nostalgia, inspiration, open palms, harmony, light, a lifted face, beauty, freedom, flexibility, curiosity, possibility and potential, growth, bliss, wholeness, compromise, building bridges, reaching out and rising up, well-being, ease, aspirations, grief and loss, and connection to and with self/other people/ animals/football teams/careers/buildings/objects/gardens/small plastic replicas of Star Wars characters/mobile phone handsets… anything.

Connection endlessly, gently produces the warm, sweet, sticky glue that holds your internal and external worlds together and needs nothing in return. It's the expansive lens through which you relate to everything with relaxed openness, enjoyment and acceptance, knowing problems will blow over, that things can only get better and that, whichever way the cards fall, you're going to be okay. It fills you up and is where you're happy and whole from within. It's the engine within you that always 'can'.

Probably the most powerful and familiar connection word you use is 'love', which I'll talk about in detail in Principle 2. Connection through loving and being loved both trigger the connection part of your brain. Whichever you do, it's all good when you're in connection. This is the win–win that creates and sustains communities, marriages, families, societies, Tinder and Comic-Con, and generally makes the world such a great place to be.

In terms of feelings, connection contains empathy, love, grief (grief being love with no place to go), safety, affection, appreciation, peace, gratitude, calmness, kindness, warmth, acceptance, forgiveness, compassion, trust, pride and hope for self and others. Behaviourally, you live it in grand gestures and in

We usually meet our needs

BOTTOM UP

 3. CONNECTION

 2. REWARD

 **1. SAFETY**

the slightest, sweetest moments: a warm smile, the light touch of your hand, your gentle sigh on a sunny day.

Connection's boundless, unlimited resource works particularly well when you couple it with reward, i.e. you're eating, working towards, having sex with and building a life with, and around, what you love. Because connection feelings are so pleasurable, reward will work effortlessly to sustain and reinforce them. Their double act is the source of endless songs, pictures, babies, landscaped gardens and bonsai trees. It gives you the best reasons why and why not and is where you experience true meaning and purpose in life; moved by an infinite carrot, rather than the stick of threat. You can see that connection and threat are a thousand light years away from each other. While threat takes apart, identifies flaws and the reasons why not, connection brings together and builds.

However, because of the reward you get from it, connection in the form of love of others has the same potential as threat and reward to cause you a problem if it becomes dominant. You can see this happening if you've fallen, or remained, in love with someone, when, on balance, this is unhelpful for your self-care. There is the struggle of 'love addiction', where someone has a constant, overwhelming compulsion towards an unhealthy dependency on 'loved ones', to the detriment of themselves and the relationship. Mainly though, connection should be prefaced by a resounding 'helpful'.

Balance

You can see that all three parts of the brain provide their own different, vital contributions to you living a great life. It's important to bear in mind that the needs they meet are met in a logical hierarchy within you, from the bottom up: your safety first (you can't eat or date people if you're dead), then, it seems to me, most often reward next (you can't take care of anyone if you don't eat), then connection. Connection always defers to threat to avoid an actual physical, or imagined, problem. Try to keep in mind, therefore, that threat, for safety reasons, is always going to be the place you **have to** start at first. It's not that you're a selfish person or different to anybody else when you do this, you just

In connection we feel

CONNECTED

and

REWARDED

and

SAFE

can't see that others are doing it too. What we're focusing on in this book is **only staying in threat for the shortest period of time that you need to**. Bear in mind also that, when you're in it, connection meets **all** needs 'top down' – you'll feel connected, rewarded and safe all at the same time when living in connection. This is why we all so yearn for this connected state.

Once threat and reward are largely met, you'll naturally always be looking upwards to connection. You can see this at work in people who might have married someone largely based on their physical appearance (reward/status reward need) or who wasn't very loving but had money, power and status (threat and status reward needs) and was a 'good provider'. After some time of these safety and reward needs being consistently met, this person, with their threat focus on what's lacking, often then starts to wonder what it would be like to have the next step up in the hierarchy of their needs met – a real loving connection with their partner. At this point they'll look expectantly to someone dominated by status reward to be a connected, loving partner and possibly parent. Unsurprisingly, they're often going to be disappointed. Even if they wanted to, a relentless money-making machine may struggle to turn quickly enough into connected lover just because their partner, or a baby, wants/needs them to.

On the subject of a balanced connection, when choosing a 'romantic' partner, or even friends, try to bear in mind how that person fares in maintaining connection. How many of us consciously think about how, and how well, the other person soothes themselves, for example, or how grateful, patient or empathetic they are in everyday life, or how intimately they know their internal landscape and patterns, when we're choosing to be in a long-term relationship with them? Perhaps if we worked towards more 'conscious coupling', we'd be able to spend less time working out how to 'consciously uncouple'. I'd also suggest that you don't base conclusions on what either of you are like during the involuntary stage of falling in love – this is often not anyone's default way of being. In the same way as when the 'fallen in love' state with someone has worn off, you'll usually, with your biases, lack the benefit of involuntary connection with them, when you're in the fallen in love state,

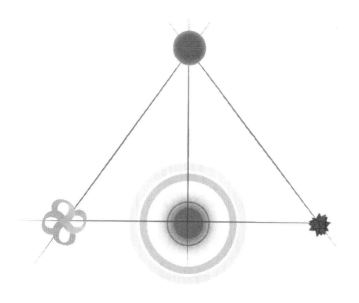

a balanced
connection

you may lack the benefit of helpful threat when looking at them.

Clearly applying threat more than we need to, lacking the capacity to helpfully filter experience, would be so painful and even often at odds with reality, that it only makes sense to use it for 'real' problems. Why put threat's sometimes paranoid, jerky, unempathetic victim in charge of internal and external relationships and therefore our well-being? We know the problems of a life controlled by reward, so why metaphorically bleed to death for 'never enough'? The ideal set-up is for threat, reward and connection to work together for the common good, for them to be in **balance**. You need to be a jack of all three parts, **mastered by none**. By maintaining balance, you can meet your safety, satisfaction/reward and connection needs, without experiencing too much fear and anger (symptoms of unmet safety need), frustration and craving (symptoms of unmet reward need) and heartache (symptom of unmet connection need). Threat makes sure you sit somewhere safe, reward makes sure it's in the sun, threat puts your sun protection on and connection means you'll relax and be grateful for the experience.

If you want the greatest power you can have in this lifetime, **it's to have this power over your three parts**. Power over yourself. To handle other people well, to handle life well, you need to handle yourself well. In doing this, by establishing and maintaining **balance** between your parts, you really can have all you need. You'll be able to tolerate the pain that comes from occupying threat without struggling with it and experience the pleasure of reward and connection without having to engage in them compulsively. You'll see that, in balance, connection will need to dominate, with some fun, reward and drive added to get you up every day and a sprinkling of threat aversion to stop you walking in front of buses.

When threat's too dominant, you're probably looking at 50/30/20 in terms of the threat/reward/connection proportions. If it's reward that is controlling you, you're looking at 30/50/20. When your proportions are in balance, taking into account the low levels of **actual** threat, it will look more like 10/30/60. It is because connection forms the biggest part in

treat - negative bias
reward - moment of satisfaction
connection — love, care, togetherness

19

this balance that establishing and maintaining a '**balanced connection**' is the main aim of this book.

Just a final word on these proportions. I can hear some people say that it's okay that they're different and change as they go through life. Young people, for example, may be used to a much greater focus on status reward/drive in friendship groups and occupy it more in the early stages of their career, and that's fine because they can change over time. Certainly, in earlier stages of life, a focus on status reward can lead to an accumulation of wealth that makes a connected life easier to maintain later on. I'd add a note of helpful threat to this though – on the basis we're habit-forming creatures, largely programmed to do in the future what we've done in the past, you should at least be curious about how these proportions are going to change if and when the time comes. For example, if a spouse and children are part of your future plan, how are you going to make the necessary move from being dominated by reward/drive to connection that's going to make this a largely enjoyable experience? Of course, you may, involuntarily, fall in love with your baby and it'll be a non-issue, but what if this doesn't happen? You'll struggle to soothe a crying baby at 2am if you're yearning to be five shots of tequila down on a beach in Thailand.

Try to make sure the transition is as smooth as it can be by keeping an eye on what parts you're putting your energy into **throughout** your life, and bear in mind that, at any age, connection is the part that meets all of your needs 'top down' and therefore provides the most sustainable happiness.

Based on the problems of allowing threat, reward and even connection free reign, it seems to be a no-brainer to operate more in balance, but, for various reasons, your proportions may have become unbalanced without you being aware of it, causing the issues that have brought you to this book. We'll now explore the signs to look out for if you're being dominated by either threat or reward, or both.

CHAPTER 2

Signs You Need More Connection

You might be distressed because, without really knowing it, you're living in threat, reacting from it to most things, **believing you're much less safe than you actually are. Your brain and body might too often be set to being afraid**, your existence too often being about self-preservation. As a result, you may be either chronically over-aroused or under-aroused (when your system is just too tired of the relentless threat activity and gives up), working **for** threat rather than the other way around, like having a boss you hate. Or you might be spending too much time in reward, bored and frustrated with yourself and life unless you're eating, exercising, drinking, on your phone, watching TV or buying more stuff you don't really need.

Most of us don't know that we're actually existing this way, but the big names of anxiety, depression, anger management, co-dependence and narcissism are all warning signs that you're living too much in threat and addictions indicate that you're too dominated by reward. I explain these in more detail in Chapter 3 (page 37).

Signs of dominant threat/reward in relationship with self

• Because threat only identifies problems and has no capacity to soothe or value you, your life can be defined by what you perceive you 'lack'. You might therefore be described as a 'perfectionist', engaging in constant 'self-improvement' because you're never quite good enough for yourself and have expectations of yourself and others that rarely make allowances for humanity. You might also describe yourself as a 'control freak' and/or a 'glass half empty' person.

DOMINANT THREAT

rumination

no purpose

loneliness

depression

hopelessness

narcissism

anxiety

imposter syndrome

chronic anger

procrastination

perfectionism

co-dependence

- Because you continuously identify problems you might struggle to land on solutions and prioritise steps forward in life, leading to procrastination and/or rumination when trying to make decisions. The fear of change and/or 'failure' and/or commitment can sometimes be paralysing with your tendency to err on the side of caution.
- As threat sees the problem in anything it looks at and is the place of anger at self, when viewing your past, you'll see the problem in any decision you've made to date. You might often therefore feel regretful and wish you had a crystal ball for the future.
- Because of threat's problem focus and its preoccupation with comparisons and difference, you might believe you're not like other people. Threat is unfortunately comparing your **internal experience** to someone else's **external appearance**, usually in a social environment, which can lead to you forming this impression.
- As threat/reward are only about survival/the next rewarding experience respectively, you might have little idea of what you actually want and, even, who you are outside of this.
- Threat's constant worry might mean you stop yourself saying what you want to say and doing what you want to do.
- Threat's problem focus will mean you're likely to have low self-esteem/worth/confidence, which can result in you at times being 'high maintenance' or 'needy'. I believe threat is the 'inner critic' inside all of us.
- Because you're not always a good friend to yourself, you may not like being alone. You're likely to find doing 'nothing' difficult. Times when there's no outward-in stimulation to take you away from your threat/inner critic, for example night-times or early mornings, can be especially hard.
- Low self-worth means you might believe you're 'stupid', 'lazy', 'crazy', 'fucked up', 'a loser' or 'a failure'.
- At work, you might have 'imposter syndrome' – a belief that you can't actually do the job you're doing well at all and it's only a matter of time before you get found out.
- Due to threat's outward-in bias, problem-finding and the lack of self-confidence, you might often look outside for the way forward, lacking trust in your own decisions and instinct.

DOMINANT REWARD

always comparing

addiction

constant yearning

constant striving

better/less than

dependency

always competing

endless novelty

compulsions

relentless acquisition

never enough

- You might compensate for low self-worth by overcompensating both in your behaviour and your imagination, for example, feeling superior/needing to be better than others, having a 'big ego', boasting/bragging/'humblebragging', showing off or being hyper-competitive. Hyper-competitiveness is also a characteristic of those controlled by reward.

- Because the present moment, untouched, is never going to be good enough for problem-focused threat/reward, you might think the 'grass is always greener', have a 'fear of missing out' (FOMO) and/or often think you should be doing something else/more or that 'there must be more to life than this'. This is where envy may come in as a threat feeling.

- Because threat thoughts are intrusive and can be obsessive, relentless and unpleasant, you'll probably say you 'over-think', are 'in your head' too much or describe yourself as a 'worrier'. You might also say you need to be 'distracted' from your thoughts.

- Dominant threat/reward can cause huge problems for your body, such as lack of sleep, overeating and chronic stress and anxiety, as you'll see in detail in Principle 4 (page 93).

- As threat is also not the place of your conscious memory and clear thinking, you might struggle to recall events from years ago or focus attention on tasks in the present.

- Threat's preoccupation with danger might mean you often have a nagging sense that something will go wrong at some point. In fact, you might believe that if you look forward to something, you're always going to be disappointed.

- Due to threat's short-term self-preservation state, you're unlikely to be putting much energy into imagining a future. Your life's 'long game' is of no interest to threat. It worries only about your immediate safety; avoiding death, not enhancing your potential life.

- Threat's victim perspective might mean you believe you're unlucky or cursed.

- You might recognise a pattern that things often don't turn out as bad as you thought they would, i.e. threat's catastrophising is making mountains out of molehills. Looking back, you'll have often worried about things that you don't even remember a year on.

- Because anger is often next to threat's fear, you might be 'an angry person', 'moody', 'short-fused', 'impatient', 'fiery', 'feisty', a 'bad sport' and/or experience 'road rage'. You're likely to easily express anger, but find it difficult to tell others you love them and mean it.

- As threat only ever finds problems, is only ever about survival and never gives up, you might feel overwhelmed, lost or drained, or that you're 'running on empty', in a 'rat race', 'going through the motions' or disenchanted, and experience a lack of meaning and purpose in your life.

- If your physiological response to threat is over-arousal, you'll be restless and say you 'can't sit still', are 'always on the go' and 'can't meditate'. If it's under-arousal, you'll often be bored, despairing and apathetic. More on under- and over-arousal later.

- Threat's jerky reactivity might lead you to believe life/love is a 'rollercoaster'.

Signs of dominant threat/reward in relation to others and your wider environment

- Because threat most often narrates your experience of yourself and others and only sees the 'flaws', you'll often judge, criticise, 'grief troll' and complain about and around others, even expect rejection from them and assume you'll be disliked.

- Because of threat's victim/perpetrator dynamic, you might often feel lonely and marooned and think you're being marginalised, disempowered, victimised, bullied, slighted, undervalued, and/or taken for granted – that the whole world's against you and you don't belong anywhere. You might then often feel shame and embarrassment as a result.

- You might believe people are watching you/talking about you much more than they actually are. You'll care far too much about someone just looking at you sideways.

- You may be suspicious and cynical about others' motives, think the worst of them, have 'trust issues' and believe people intend to hurt others far more than they actually do.

- Your low self-worth, fear and the outward-in preoccupation mean that, as difficult as you find them, you may need constant reassurance from other people. You may volunteer for lots in order to please others, but then find yourself resenting all the commitments.

- You might preoccupy too much about what other people think about you, about 'proving yourself' to others, about what you said or should have said in situations, and about social media 'likes' or popularity as a result. You might even come off social media because it 'makes' you feel bad about yourself.

- Along with your self-image, your view of others is likely to go from zero to hero, and back, in a short period of time as you're jerked around too much by fear/anger.

- In the same way that threat's problem- and self-preservation-focus means you'll take yourself for granted, you may have a tendency to do this with others.

- Because of the lack of self-worth and outward-in focus, if it appears someone seems to really understand you, remembers you, sees you and cares about you, it's surprising and therefore a big deal to you. You might notice you get a significant 'contact high' from it.

- As we'll discuss later, due to persistent fear, you might be avoidant of confrontation, submissive and/or lack assertiveness and therefore be two-faced sometimes. Due to threat's anger, you might also have a tendency with others to want to 'destroy them before they destroy you' and be overly confrontational with them.

- Anger's resistance to yielding, coupled with a fear of the unknown, means you may struggle to say you're sorry to a loved one, but apologise needlessly to strangers.

- As threat's self-preservation state can't afford to be tolerant, lacks empathy and is often annoyed, you might gossip a lot, condemn others, play people off against each other, harshly judge them, be resentful, have feuds, hold grudges and struggle to forgive. Threat will want to make other people 'pay' and to hold them to account.

- Due to a heightened focus on your external environment, you might give uninvited opinions and be unclear as to what's your business and within your power/control and what isn't.

- The constant fear means you might have a tendency to bring conversations about others back to you. You can look self-centred, but you're just much more concerned than you need to be about self-preservation.

- Again, due to persistent fear, you may be phobic of things/ behaviours and, adding anger to this, even phobic of particular groups of people: the rich, the poor, the political right, the political left, men, women, gay people, straight people, the police, Americans, the government, etc. You might experience them like a homogenous mass of 'they', rather than as groups of individual human beings.

- Due to threat's problem-focus and biases, you might believe familiarity breeds contempt and have fewer friends than you'd like and/or have quite a number of ex-friends who you believe treated you 'badly'.

- Because threat finds the problem in everything and has little sense of (yours and) others' goodness, you might believe that to talk to others about your problems will 'burden' them.

- Threat's catastrophising and biases mean you might generally believe this world is 'going to hell in a handcart'. People have been predicting the end of civilisation since civilisation began.

You can see from the above that your experience of yourself and others can get sucked into the black hole of threat. If you have such a painful psychological toothache, you'll struggle to think about anything else and, as you can only think, feel and do one thing at a time, you can't also be in connection. Because of the hierarchy in which your needs are met, the loser in threat/ reward will therefore always be your connection with self and others. As time goes on, connection may quietly shrink and, with it, your expansive thought, feeling and behavioural energy. Your capacity to feed and nurture yourself and others might diminish as a result. With much of the space, joy and breath being sucked out of life in the process.

You may, understandably, be employing reward concurrently with threat to relieve the pain of this lack of connection: bringing sex, food, winning and competing against others for resources, along with other behaviours and substances that mimic their effect, further into your life to temporarily make you feel better. Reward isn't connection though, so, although you might often look, and be, highly driven and productive, by spending even more time out of connection, you'll be perpetuating your lack of safety and contentment and feeding threat/reward.

Where does dominant threat/reward come from?

A number of factors mean that you'll naturally be dominated by threat if you don't deliberately do something different. Primarily, as you know, it's meant to be the all-powerful part. Your personal security didn't see it enter, because it **is** your personal security. You may have existed with pervasive threat so early in childhood that you don't even notice it now. Experiences that often lead to occupying threat/reward more than is helpful for us include:

- having caregivers who modelled it
- being bullied
- being sent to boarding school
- prolonged illness as a child
- sexual/emotional/physical abuse/neglect
- being intrinsically 'different' in a way you can't, and shouldn't have to, change (even if you tried, even if you wanted to), but are led to believe is pathological, for example, a minority sexuality and/or gender identity, having a disability and/or autistic spectrum disorder and/or attention deficit hyperactivity disorder/attention deficit disorder

The most common factor that I see with my clients from the above list is having caregivers who modelled threat/reward and who were therefore often frightened/frightening/numb/emotionally absent and/or addicted. You can see, though, that if any of the other factors listed above, or a combination of them, were present when you were growing up, they're likely to have led to you feeling far less safe than you should have, turning threat right up and, often, concurrently, reward to deal with it. Much of the explanation below is therefore in a large part also applicable to the other factors listed above. It's important to say at this point that none of what follows is intended to be about blaming caregivers. Most are just doing their best based on what they learned from their own caregivers, and so on. They will most likely also have modelled some qualities and behaviours that are really helpful for you in life now and it's important to acknowledge these too. However, we do need to look at any adverse effects that their 'care' might have had on you.

If you had childhood caregivers who were controlled by, and therefore modelled, threat/reward this is how things are for you, just because that's how it's always been. The more you've used threat/reward's beliefs and assumptions, the more they'll have been played out and built on as your life has gone on. Your brain will automatically notice, prioritise and remember experiences that confirm your pre-existing beliefs, no matter how distressing they are for you. This is known as your 'confirmation bias'. If you get a threat story in your head about someone 'using' you, for example, without you even being conscious of it, you'll **only** be looking for, even imagining, information that supports this distressing belief. Dominant threat/reward may have sunk into your unconscious, tainting the automatic assumptions you make and the set of beliefs you follow, invisible to you now, except for the reasons you're reading this book.

Your brain developed most significantly during your early years and adolescence. You were born mainly with basic threat and reward, lots of fear and impulses, with the rest of your brain designed to be filled up by your caregivers. Humans have an unmatched capacity to be imprinted on during childhood: mainly a long process of the world telling you how to think, feel and behave. Your young brain was designed to be 'easily led', to be made to take on the systems, values, rules, goals and beliefs that enabled you to fit in with your caregivers and the wider environment, safeguarding your survival as part of the group/family. This all makes evolutionary sense, as we're stronger if we stick together from a survival perspective.

Being completely dependent on, and open to being programmed by, your environment would have been all good if balanced connection was modelled in secure, consistent relationships with connected, loving caregivers. Loving looks from caregivers are the most important boost to the growth of our social brain. If loving connection was regularly present, as well as feeling safe and enjoying yourself, you'd have been shown how to healthily regulate yourself (including your thoughts, feelings and body) and tolerate distress, by self-soothing/comforting to remain connected internally and externally. It's worth noting here that you regulate yourself in one of two ways: either on your own (for example, exercise, food, yoga) or by being in relationships with others. You need to be able to do **both** to maintain balanced connection, as you'll come to see.

Many of us actually have caregivers who are controlled by threat/reward, because that's the most likely pattern humans form due to our brain structure. And because, as you've seen, threat's self-preservation state means lots of fear, anger and shame, coupled with a lack of empathy for, and attunement with, others, if that's where your caregivers were, that's what you'd have most likely faced. You may even **only** have got eye contact – and angry eye contact at that – when you were doing something 'wrong'. And because threat sees difference as threatening, difference from your caregivers in opinions, preferences and behaviours would probably have been deemed 'wrong' or 'bad' behaviour.

This would have left you feeling unsafe, turning threat up in your brain, which had no real strategies yet for soothing itself. You unfortunately had no ability as a child to gauge the degree of severity of any perceived threat and couldn't therefore put a caregiver's angry face into perspective as something that would just blow over in time. Your natural dependence also meant your caregiver's behaviour and demeanour were exaggerated in your young mind. This will have combined with your brain's negativity bias to automatically move mainly distressing experiences to your 'below the radar' core memories. It's these core memories that form your sense of who you, others and the world are.

Healthy ways to self-soothe/comfort and regulate yourself back to connection in relationships with other people – like validating and empathising with your hurt feelings, talking yourself gently through your fear/anger and calming you – wouldn't

31

have been modelled often enough by someone who lacked the ability to do this for themselves. You were probably then only left with, and expected to use, the most easily to hand of the self-regulating behaviours, like sugary foods or buying more stuff, that can, over time, become unhelpful coping behaviours.

You can imagine that the volume of threat feelings and sadness might have become overwhelming for you in this situation. Lacking the ability to self-soothe, you'd then have had little choice but to distance yourself from your feelings. In the process, you may have lost your handle on feelings and how to process them helpfully.

From a neuroscientific point of view, the cortisol – a stress hormone – released when we're in threat shrinks the brain's hippocampus – the part of your brain that calms your amygdala. Without a sizeable hippocampus, you'll have found it more difficult to put things in context later in life. For example, you unconsciously identify your raging partner as an angry caregiver/parent and you tiptoe around, trying desperately not to upset them as you'd have done with your caregiver as a child. This is rather than discussing with them calmly, adult to adult, how things might be different. Or when your partner/friend looks at their phone while you're talking to them, they unconsciously become the mother controlled by threat who wasn't really interested in who you were as an individual, just as an extension of her and so you go, as you did as an adolescent, into a passive-aggressive 'mood', which unfortunately changes nothing. Your capacity to distinguish past, present and future in such moments will have been compromised. And with it, therefore, your ability to say, 'Well that was terrible when it happened, but thank goodness it's over now.'

As you were dependent on your caregivers for survival as a child, you couldn't just leave the metaphorical room. You even had to **go towards** the threat/reward caregiver, despite experience telling you that at times it wasn't safe: your only source of comfort was the source of heartbreak. **Fear and love would therefore inevitably have merged into each other. Fearing the person/people that you need and want**, you'd have **connected traumatically, the experience of loving always coupled with an underlying insecurity**. It would have been frightening both to leave the relationship and to stay in it, an experience that would then have been carried through into your adult relationships with your brain's confirmation bias. This may lead you to always be one foot in and one foot out in romantic relationships in particular, or avoidant of them altogether ('commitment phobes'), or even co-dependent (see page 43).

As a child you would have needed to make sense of the predicament described above to live with your caregivers in the way you had to to survive. With no competing narrative available and, therefore, no way of knowing that threat/reward caregivers should, and could, have behaved differently, this would have left only you to blame for all the threat feelings experienced by all parties. It would also have been less frightening for you to believe you were in the wrong, and/or defective, than for there to be a problem with the person you were completely dependent on for survival. Your internal environment would have become filled with toxic blame and shame directed towards self.

The caregiver controlled by threat will also likely have enforced and perpetuated this blame of you as a child with their reluctance to take responsibility (see Principle 1). Your self would have gone into hiding from the world, because, and quite rightly with threat/reward caregivers, you didn't believe anyone would understand. Your caregiver may also have looked to you to take care of their needs, to soothe them. This is something you would, of course, have tried to do, but it would have put your own needs and wants further out of sight.

And that's how you then organise experience from childhood on. With neural pathways that suggest there's something a bit shameful/defective about you. That you're of little value and unlovable, unless you're pleasing your caregiver. Threat's your dominant experience, its reactivity wired-in to consistently fire up when there's no need, or with an under-aroused system because you understandably gave up on listening and responding to your feelings. Maybe you go between both. Stuck in your confirmation bias, even despite some evidence to the contrary as you've grown. Like those trees that grow horizontally in the direction the wind has always blown – looking incongruous, stuck in a moment, still so beaten down even on a calm, sunny day.

The dominant threat/reward double act

Adding to its power, as mentioned above, to try to reduce its pain, threat may have commandeered reward. Living in threat is uncomfortable and understandably your brain looks for ways to return to balance. With a past, present and future filled only with threat's problems and the contentment offered by connection largely unavailable, reward provides the only quick-to-hand relief. In fact, because they involve similar chemicals, a lot of us actually **mistake reward for connection**. If you do that, though, you're confusing the glitter of temporary reward with the gold of real connection. You might have developed habits of using sex, food, winning, competing with others and other endorphin (your body's natural psychological and physical pain-killer) and dopamine-inducing substances and behaviours to escape and reduce threat thoughts and feelings that you believe you can't tolerate. Often, therefore, **the problems now, were the solutions then**; at one point dominant threat/reward were helpful adaptations to deal with the situation you had no choice but to be in.

As I mentioned above, if you're using the threat/reward double act, you might be trying to live a life that's 'better than', or superior to, others', to escape threat's inescapable delusion that you're worth very little. As threat shines the light exclusively on flaws and problems, whatever you acquire or achieve won't satisfy you in the long term. **You** will never be enough. There's always someone out there with something you don't have. Threat/reward is never done doing, acquiring or comparing, forever yearning for something lacked. You won't enjoy the things you do have, because within minutes of getting something, your attention will have moved to the things you don't, or imagine you don't, have.

Another trick of a threat/reward combination is also that, because of all the fun you've been having in reward, your levels of threat might often have been masked. It might look to you and to others like you're actually having a great time. However, happiness in the form of peace, contentment and satisfaction is structurally mission impossible when controlled by the dominant threat/reward double act. True happiness will come only from being mostly in connection. While existing in excessive threat, the best you'll get is relief from anxiety. Relief that the thing you dreaded happening (which threat most likely catastrophised and imagined anyway) hasn't happened. Thank goodness that slight tension headache wasn't a brain tumour after all, that you got 85 per cent in that exam you knew you'd definitely failed or that she's not in fact cheating on you, she's just having a stressful time at work. Living a life controlled by reward, you'll get just the fleeting highs that follow eating a sugary snack, getting a more expensive car than your neighbour or bagging that twentieth pair of shoes.

The power of imagination

Threat/reward are also made stronger by our imagination (see Principle 6 for more on this). Human imagination has created a very complicated environment that we're now expected to navigate. Early human experience wasn't about much more than survival and procreation. Now we have the Internet, reality TV and social media, religious, political and social systems all buzzing around a stimulating and noisy world.

If you apply your imagination to connection and helpful reward, you can imagine endless heart-warming and exciting scenarios. If you apply imagination to unhelpful reward, though, you'll have the persistent fantasy that can make cravings difficult to resist, known as 'euphoric recall' – the, often intrusive, images of the most pleasurable times when you engaged in the relevant behaviour or substance, without any recollection of the bad times. And, applied to threat, your imagination gives you access to a viewing library of every distressing scenario you've heard of, real or imagined. Everyone else's horror stories are pulled in and made yours. Netflix and anything but chill. Your imagination can, as we'll see in Principle 6, either beautifully serve and perpetuate balanced connection in your life or, in the hands of threat/ reward, be your worst enemy.

Contemporary culture

Because many of us are actually living with dominant threat/ reward, they also dominate contemporary culture. They've sunk into your unconscious and therefore go unchallenged. The media, advertising, fitness, self-development, risk and compliance, medical, marketing, journalism, sports, fashion and legal indus-tries, even therapy, might all coexist with and perpetuate threat/reward in various ways. Marketing points your attention towards what you don't have; law preoccupies with identifying problems and loopholes; sports has its relentless competiveness defining 'success' as winning; and fashion implicitly attaches your worth and value to what others can see.

Worse than operating under the radar of your conscious scrutiny, threat/reward may also have been rewarded in life. Even despite experiencing the threat/reward conditions I describe in Chapter 3, they may have meant you're conscientious to the point of martyrdom, perfectionist, compliant and therefore a highly rewarded partner, friend and employee. You might be distressed, but you're probably well paid. Which is, of course, what's most important to threat/reward.

It's worth bearing in mind that the situation for men may be even more challenging here. For physiological reasons, the tendency to anger is quicker. Add to this that aggression can be respected, rewarded, even encouraged, as men go through life. Prioritising being in connection is not part of the 'men's code'. By the time they've left primary school, most boys have taken in the message that it's better to die than show the 'weakness' of being hurt or a need for loving connection. And, at their own hands via suicide, they more often do.

Finally, as well as the self-fulfilling prophecy causing threat to tighten up by feeding itself over time, threat believes, whatever the problem is, that it's permanent, with no possibility of change. This also adds to the hopelessness and helplessness you might feel when trying to change this situation. Ways to overcome these threat mind tricks by managing your thoughts and beliefs are outlined in Principle 4.

CHAPTER 3

Conditions That Stem from Dominant Threat/Reward

From the examples you've seen so far, you may recognise some thoughts, feelings and behavioural characteristics of living in threat/reward, or certainly that you're occupied by these two parts more often than is helpful/necessary for you. As they have such a profound effect on us it's not surprising we've also developed names for what I believe are conditions that stem from being dominated by threat/reward: addiction, anxiety and stress, depression, anger, narcissism and co-dependency.

As you'll see, because of their threat/reward common roots, these conditions overlap much more than is often acknowledged. Although 'an anxious person' can look and feel very different to 'an angry person', I think they're both manifestations of dominant threat. As the root's the same, what helps the addicted helps the depressed, the anxious, the angry, etc., which you can also see from the cross-prescription of antidepressant medication for depression, anxiety and even addictions.

Anger

We know that the unchecked, reactive threat behaviours that follow anger can result in homicides and suicides. But, just like the threat feeling of fear/anxiety, anger (and annoyance, irritation, frustration and rage are all on the 'anger scale') can be as helpful as all other feelings in getting your emotional needs and wants met. If, for example, you notice a pattern of getting annoyed around someone who's taking you down in social situations, it's probably important for your connection with self that you take notice of it and act on it. Calling them an 'arsehole' in a moment of anger though is reactive anger; speaking **from** anger rather than **for** it. It will probably just make things worse and even leave you needing to apologise to someone who was actually treating you badly. Your anger's helpful message is lost here. We'll explore how to express threat feelings more helpfully in Principle 10 (page 169).

It's important to understand that anger is a boundary emotion and therefore can be an ally. You can see from the example above that anger tells you someone is crossing over your boundaries (see Principle 9) and that something is happening to you, or others, that needs to change. Like fear, it's most often protective and preoccupied with your safety. In the case of someone repeatedly taking you down, anger is the secondary emotion racing quickly in after fear, hurt, shame or a sense of injustice, to, quite rightly, encourage you to do something about the difficult situation you find yourself in. In this way, anger can be energising, protective and motivating.

However, anger might become a problem for you when you react rather than respond to it and also let it rule, unchecked, as part of living in threat. As with fear, the chronic anger of dominant threat will distort and corrupt your experience of yourself and your world. And, as with all threat feelings, you're programmed to believe and act on its messages. Your anger believes 'I'm right, you're wrong', sees only in black and white and positions the other person as perpetrator and you as victim. As we've seen with threat generally, it necessarily lacks empathy for, and dehumanises, the other. Your anger just wants you to beat them and get rid of the 'threat' so you can feel safe again.

To add to its strength, again probably for sensible evolutionary reasons, you also get a short-term reward in your brain for aggressively expressing anger. You need to bear in mind though that, although calling your partner a bitch/bastard might light a pleasurable green light in your brain for 10 seconds, they'll remember it for the rest of their lives.

As we'll see with depression, anger turned inwards also separates you from yourself. Unchecked anger directed outwards can result in the death of another person; unchecked internal anger can result in your own death through illness or suicide. I'll talk more about relating to self with love instead of fear/anger in Principle 3 (page 83).

As well as the noisy, destructive drama of reactive, unchecked anger, you also need to be aware of the other, less obvious, but just as unproductive, ways you might express anger. If, when you're angry, you're passive-aggressive, go quiet to annoy the other person or do the opposite of what you know they want you to do to get 'even', these can disconnect you from the other person just as much as angry verbal abuse. Although more sneaky than throwing plates around, they're equally messy and indiscriminate ways to show your distress. At least if you shout, someone knows you're angry. Just deliberately coming home late from work for a week because you're annoyed will confuse and irritate your partner, but ultimately achieve nothing.

You therefore need to try to avoid consistently reacting **while** you're angry, unless you want to spend your life saying sorry or enjoy prison food. The chronic reactive anger that can characterise living in threat just doesn't work when we've evolved to band together in social groups. Although, as ever, it's trying to protect you, threat anger makes you less safe by breaking connections in relationships and possibly even results in your physical harm.

Anger seems to me to be the most denied feeling. You might even struggle to say the words 'I'm angry'. Instead, you might say you're feeling 'defensive', 'tired', 'moody', 'stressed', 'upset', 'cross', 'frustrated', 'triggered' and 'grumpy'. Anger therefore seems to be more often disconnected from and hidden by shame than other feelings. It may also be less culturally acceptable in women, as is the case with sadness, fear and hurt in men. The trouble is, as with threat generally, if you're not connected to it, you're going to find it difficult to manage it, or often even be aware that you're feeling it.

The balanced connection way to relate to your anger is, as with all feelings, to notice you're feeling it, take some time to decide its message and then work out **whether**, and how, you speak **for** it to get your needs met in the situation.

Anxiety and Stress

This is the condition most commonly and easily associated with threat, where the threat feeling of fear (which includes excessive worry, doubt, nervousness, embarrassment, shame, stress, panic, anxiety and dread) dominates life. The fear might be general, or attach to something specific that depends on your life experience to date, for example, your personal physical or mental health, the health of any kids you might have, any aspect of your physical appearance/body generally, germs, or the quality of your current romantic relationship.

Attachment and Addiction

As I mentioned above, addictions, compulsions – it may even be called 'bonding' now – are conditions associated with living a life controlled by reward. I'll use the term 'addiction' from this point, for ease. Addiction is an attachment to any behaviours, or substances, that you might:

- struggle to control your use of;
- need more of over time to achieve the same effect; and
- continue to do/use, in spite of problems.

The 'problems' are key here. As you know, we under-standably dislike physical and emotional pain and look for ways to escape from and avoid it, to bring us back to balance. We're also programmed to go for the shortest way possible to achieve this – we have an inbuilt natural human preference for reward's quick, short-term gain over connection's long-term well-being and satisfaction. It's great sometimes to live life like there's no tomorrow. The trouble is, if we do that all the time – with reward controlling us, rather than the other way around – it can make for a terrible tomorrow, or even no tomorrow.

With less connection than you need, you might therefore have become attached to anything which triggers reward and helps you to feel better temporarily. As I've said, sometimes, rather than over-arousal, the result of living in threat can be under-arousal, which you might also know as boredom, apathy or depression. This'll also lead you to look outwards for stimulation to feel something, anything.

The range of behaviours and substances people get addicted to shows our vast human imagination. There are over 50 different 12-step groups dealing with everything from alcohol to shoplifting. You know the usual suspects: alcohol, drugs, sugar, caffeine, gambling, video gaming, cigarettes, 'love' and the silent epidemic of porn/sex addiction. But there's also: power, winning, work, exercise, social media, needing the constant novelty of new people, things and experiences, handheld media devices, and the relentless acquisition of money and objects.

All these potentially addictive behaviours and substances trigger reward, for some because Mother Nature sensibly rewards you for doing them – such as sex, getting new stuff, winning, exercise and eating – and, for others, because they're a chemical compound – for example, crystal meth – specifically made to do this. By triggering reward to change your stressed or numb state, chemicals including dopamine, serotonin and endorphins – your 'feel good' hormones – are released. To use rewarding behaviours and substances in a balanced way is taking responsibility for your well-being, as you'll see in Principle 1, but if you're not careful, addiction can take hold. Addiction causes sustained harm and reinforces the threat state you brought it in to alter, in turn fuelling the need for more reward. And so it goes on. You might recognise this pattern if you're reading this book.

Many addictions go unnoticed because they never result in obvious problems. Often though, it's just a matter of cultural norms whether a consequence of addiction is seen as a problem or not. Take the heroin addict and the workaholic businessperson. One is looking at a criminal record, the other a six-bedroom house with a seven-car garage. If you're looking at problems, both addictions potentially cause serious physical and psychological ones for the addict and those around them – for the heroin addict this can include death by overdose; for the workaholic business person it can be meaning little more than a stressed-out blank cheque to the people they want to love and be loved by.

Why do we carry on engaging with behaviours and/or substances despite these problems? As well as neurochemical reasons, which result in frustration and cravings if we don't get the reward, often coupled with needing more and more of the substance or behaviour to achieve the same effect, psychotherapy also has something important to contribute here. Some theorists believe addictions are about 'acting out' feelings.

Acting out is a reward-seeking, impulsive type of behaviour that ignores our own and others' feelings and is harmful to connection, even safety/helpful threat. It's always useful in therapy to work on the basis that addictive impulses result from early childhood experiences that were so overwhelming we weren't able to integrate them into our developing sense of self. They therefore sit outside of our perception. I've already described the ways this might happen above (pages 29–33). Engaging in addictive behaviour without conscious feeling is described as a 'trance-like state'. Every addict has an unhealthy relationship with their feelings and body, meaning we're often not even conscious of the threat feelings of fear, shame, anger and guilt that characterise most of the cycle of addictive behaviour.

In the case of childhood attachment and trauma issues, these turn up threat and the resultant uncomfortable feelings need anaesthetising, and/or we feel so numb that our system craves some kind of arousal to feel alive. Without other more helpful ways to do either, we engage with the behaviour or substance. We then get the triple whammy of:

1. the intrinsically addictive nature of many of these behaviours and substances; combined with

2. the fact they in turn reinforce, or even create, threat/reward; combined with

3. we engage with them largely outside of our consciousness and therefore control.

By way of example, due to childhood trauma, you might exist uncomfortably in threat and so consume sugary foods to temporarily make yourself feel better. As described above though, because dominant threat makes the external environment your focus, you'll have forgotten what feelings feel like inside your body and with that, all the messages about what to come away from and what to go towards that these provide (see page 102 for more on this). Although the physiological effect of endless boxes of chocolates is momentarily fewer threat feelings and more reward, you may not actually even be conscious of what's really happening inside you. It's all happening outside of your everyday thinking/feeling. And, as your weight increases and your health deteriorates, you won't be tracking your feelings or perhaps even know of any other ways to help yourself to feel good. Instead, you might just experience a vague, nagging unease, your response to which, without other more helpful ways to connect, is to eat more chocolate and ice cream.

In the case of some addictions, for example sex, they can develop largely on the basis of opportunity. Someone who has no significant history of problematic connection and trauma can become addicted just because surfing limitless porn to the crest of the orgasm five times a day is like attaching a cocaine drip to their arm and inevitably becomes addictive. This is a minority of cases though; many of us will have past trauma and connection issues in some form or another.

And what about connection if you're an addict? It's likely that connection feelings are what you've yearned for either to soothe or to feel alive. Connection is the state you want to alter to, i.e. a sense of wholeness and/or love that, sadly, just may not have been part of your childhood caregivers' toolbox. You could see drugs, alcohol, sex or food, etc. as little liquid shots, or powdered, connection. In precious moments in the addictive cycle, you experience some connection qualities: ecstasy, intimacy, closeness to and oneness with others and self. At least for a while, there is the absence of the internal threat/reward war. This is an understandable, yet unsustainable and misdirected way to briefly occupy the connection you feel happiest in. But temporary absence of war is not the true peace of consistently occupying this part. Addictions can fuel a war that, without intervention, can eventually destroy you, with liver cirrhosis, suicide and overdoses being just a few of the ways.

Co-Dependency

Co-dependency is what I believe dominant threat looks like in relationships with others. Whereas balanced connection with another person is based on, and sustains, connection to a known and loved self, threat offers mainly frightened, angry and/or empty space **inside** of you. As we've seen, the latter prevents a grounded sense of your worth, value and lovability. Hobbling your capacity to love, even know, your shape. With the outward push of threat, you might look to others to fill this space, usually romantic partners, but also potentially children, parents and/or friends. **It's only someone else that gets you into feel-good connection with yourself.**

With co-dependency, you often look to the other person to define you and be the answer to all your threat pain/fear/ emptiness. You become reliant on them for your worth and value, your sense of who you are. Effectively a prisoner of someone else's love, you're in a co-dependent relationship.

Co-dependency can be summed up in the phrase, 'How empty of me to be so full of you.' You might believe partners are 'other halves', rather than one and one making two. You're likely to drop almost everything and everyone when you're in a co-dependent relationship. You'll put the other above you and before you, orbiting around them and expecting the same in return. Expecting them to 'protect' you from the emptiness of a self dominated by threat. Without being aware of it, you'll be looking to merge with them to calm threat's fear of difference. You can lose your sense of where you end psychologically and the other person begins, confused as to which are your feelings in any given moment and which are the other person's. 'I'm happy if you're happy' and 'Without you, there is no me' are common mantras here.

The problem with existing like this is, of course, that none of us can be everything another person needs all the time. You're asking the impossible to become one with another. You'll never feel as close as co-dependency consistently needs, no matter how tightly you hold the other person. It may work for a while, but, over time, as the initial, involuntary 'honeymoon' connection chemicals wear off and threat retakes centre stage, the inevitable differences in opinion, feelings and behaviours, seen as threats to the merger, lead to more threat feelings including jealousy and anger.

Co-dependency is a state that was only ever helpful for you as a newborn baby. At birth you were naturally enmeshed with your caregivers and relied on them for all your emotional and physical needs. When your partner, children or friends uncon- sciously become these caregivers, this is what you might expect them to become; an extension of you, there to meet your needs and sacrifice their own experience of life to meet them and vice versa. This is often without you having to explain, or even at times knowing, what your needs are. They must guess, or know, like your caregivers did when you were distressed as a baby. These are old scripts that only served an appropriate purpose a long, gone, time ago – their time has now passed.

If you're co-dependent, you get caught in the usual threat vicious circle: the more frightened and unsafe you feel, the harder you pull at the other person, forever stress- and pressure-testing the relationship, gripping it so tight it often breaks. As you know, threat feelings disconnect, so your co-dependent relationship becomes characterised by threat feelings rather than connection ones. Threat feelings lead to threat thoughts and behaviours and out of love you go, giving you even more to worry about. It's a 'can't live with them, can't live without them' relationship horror film.

Co-dependency is often, though, what you're told consti-tutes real love. Popular music sugar-coats toxic co-dependent dynamics in romantic sentiment – songs tell you how life isn't worth living without another. However, any belief that you can't exist without another person is a dominant threat illusion. Over time, it'll put unmanageable pressure on a relationship and will result either in it ending, or a really unhappy coupling. It's certainly not love. In this context, importantly, we need to look at what love actually means to you, as your definition of it may have been formed in an environment where threat/reward dominated. We'll look at this is in detail in Principle 2 (page 79).

Depression

Depression, like addiction and anxiety, is a familiar threat condition to all of us. It's important to know what we mean by the word though. You might say you're depressed when you're feeling sad or 'down'. But feeling sad, even flat sometimes, can be as much a part of feeling life as love, joy and peace.

If depression is what brings you to this book, although sadness and despair can be feelings described when someone is depressed, you know that actual depression is often not being overwhelmed by feelings, but being **underwhelmed** by them. It's the place where your response to persistent threat is largely under-arousal. Except for some anger, sadness and plenty of helplessness and hopelessness, you don't experience the range of emotions you might expect in natural response to the ups and downs of life, lacking energetic vitality. You might sound and seem flat, bored and frustrated. And you're probably, not even secretly, quite angry about this.

Although depression and anxiety can sound and feel different, because they share a threat root, they often go hand in hand. One can be present beneath the other and they feed each other. When you're depressed, you're certainly fearful, which isn't surprising given you're facing the complexities of modern life equipped with some threat hopelessness and helplessness. You'll probably mainly feel the threat feeling of anger though, rather than the anxious person's more dominant fear.

What's important here is that, unfortunately, the anger you experience mostly isn't potentially forward-moving, energetic and productive. It's not the pure, burning, transformative light of anger at injustice. Rather it can be a turgid and often debilitating anger. As writer Steve Wright said, 'it's anger without enthusiasm'.

When you're depressed, your anger machine is turned on and up and has flipped round the wrong way. You're stuck glumly in front of a tennis ball machine that keeps firing reasons at you why you're an unlucky, failing underachiever compared to others. When depression is installed, you're often too tired to even raise your racquet. Suggestions for ways forward are usually rejected. Threat anger in your imagination, and under-arousal, makes you seem determined, even eager, to close off routes out and turn them in on yourself. If your imagination wants to think of a reason why not, it'll find one.

When you're depressed, you spend little time using imagination to build your sense of self or the future you might want. You might even get annoyed if you're asked to imagine what might be different tomorrow if your depression lifted. Your threat imagination instead selects aspects of your past, present and future to keep you down. Your language might be full of buts: 'I could do that, yes, but...', 'I know I'm lucky to have my kids, but...'. **'But' negates whatever comes before**.

Characteristic of threat's victim stance is also that your sense of control over your life often sits outside of you when you're depressed. You might therefore speak in terms of 'they'. There can be a sense that malevolent external forces control your life, that you're not able to navigate your own ship. You might think and speak in threat black-and-white, binary terms, make pervasive snap judgements of pass/fail, success/failure, win/lose or good/bad, and lack awareness of shades of grey, let alone all the other colours that actually make up the world. And you're probably either numb or understandably frightened and angry about all this.

In terms of threat conditions, depression can also be more challenging to work through than anxiety. If you're anxious you'll often repeat your cycles despite interventions, but, because you're frightened, you can be soothed and it can feel good to soothe you. However, when you're depressed, the dominance of anger and despair/under-arousal, the 'help-rejecting complainer', can be more difficult for others to relate to. This can leave you more isolated than the 'simply' anxious and more likely to both think about and try suicide.

Someone once said very depressed people kill themselves because they're unable to kill the person they want to kill. The anger you turn on your self is only usually expressed outwards in an outburst, not in a way that meets your need to connect in life. You might have road rage, shout at the TV or criticise others on the Internet, but you've probably given up hope that the people you care about would change their behaviour if you asked them to.

I've explained above the story of how this can get set up. If you were reliant on caregivers controlled by threat, with whom there wasn't any point expressing anger, you'd have had lots to be angry about and nowhere for that anger to go. The writer Andrew Solomon described depression as 'like wanting to vomit, but not having a mouth'. And if it does go outwards, it can happen so forcibly (only because you were never shown how to do it helpfully) that it makes situations worse. Really the only thing you're actually hopeless and helpless against is the dominance of your own threat.

Narcissism

Based on how this word is used in everyday language, you might think narcissists are just arrogant and self-obsessed, preoccupied with themselves to the exclusion of everyone else. But, as with all these threat conditions, I think this is a frightened, self-preservation state.

One of the most helpful ways to sum up the idea of narcissism is 'special worthlessness'. If this is what brings you to this book, you'll likely be combining defensive and compensating, superior and grandiose fantasies about yourself in your imagination, with an equally imagined inferior, distorted, painful, worthless sense of self, caused by dominant threat.

Like all threat conditions, narcissism is common in our society and it's destructive. You'll largely only be using your thoughts, feelings and body to meet your own needs and wants and to maintain your imagined view of yourself. Only presidential, world-famous, King or Queen, superhero, Instagram influencer, CEO is enough. Just 'good enough' is just not good enough for you.

As I've explained with threat generally, often the more narcissistic you are, the more financially rewarded and perceived as 'successful' you are. Your drive for superior physical perfection and material wealth, along with a lack of empathy, integrity and boundaries, means you'll probably make a lot of money and show it off. You might value physical appearance, brands and conspicuous wealth, equating yours, and others', worth and value to them. Lots of selfies, a preoccupation with social media and endless cosmetic surgery might all be part of your life as a result. You might have even have got into debt chasing the illusion of superiority in having more stuff.

The promise of other people thinking you've 'made it' might have been so powerful, you sacrifice your physical and emotional well-being to achieve and sustain it. Because you're really only investing in your external image rather than your internal self, you'll also lack awareness of your feelings and we'll see in Principle 4 (page 93) why this is such a problem. You may look great and be charming at parties, but it can be a lonely and unsatisfying place to be, as you've really disconnected from much of your own humanity and therefore the humanity of others.

Children of the seventies will remember Mrs Bucket's narcissistic character in *Keeping Up Appearances*. The show was built on the premise that it's funny to value appearance over connected relationships with people, presumably because we know on some level it's ridiculous. Narcissism, like all threat/reward conditions, really isn't funny though. Intended as pain management, the reality is that it reinforces unhelpful threat/reward.

If you look at others in terms of better than, or less than, based on what they own, or what they look like, it's a disconnecting illusion. If other people see you starving yourself for a status symbol, you may also appeal only to those who see the world in the same way as you, thus creating an echo chamber in which to reinforce each other's narcissism.

As painful as it is for you, narcissism can also be painful for those who relate to you. You'll want to be loved to make it all better, but, because threat controls you, you'll lack empathy and can even be exploitative and act ruthlessly. You'll know being charming gets your needs met, but that's based on meeting your own needs rather than a genuine interest in, or appreciation of, another. It's a disorientating mix for someone else to relate to. In fact, a connected, loving relationship if you're highly narcissistic, isn't really possible. You'll only be there on your own terms. If someone isn't with you they're against you and even face some narcissistic rage. You'll be angry at what you can't rule.

So what's the source of this wound? I believe there will have been particular circumstances that mean you might exist with dominant threat/reward now. But why might you go particularly for specialness to compensate for the pain, rather than depression, anxiety or anger (although these may all be around in some form, as you'd expect)? There's interestingly a common childhood story associated with narcissism that you might recognise.

It might be that you were 'used' as a dependent child by a caregiver who had power. I often hear this about men and their mothers. The father spent most of his time disappointing the mother and she, in turn, shares her problems and wants with the son, possibly because she couldn't soothe herself any other way and/or to get her own back on the father. As a child, you'd have experienced yourself as special and superior as a result, and your powerful parent would have explicitly reinforced this.

The problem is that, if this happened, you were being used. To be in an adult's world means you have to give up childhood freedom of expression – your ability to get angry, make mistakes and to cry too. Your parent will have suggested it's because they love you so much, but this isn't really love, as we'll see in Principle 2. You didn't have any choice as a child – it was either agree or be rejected by the powerful parent. The fact that this all meant you weren't actually seen for who you were as a child – just something to make your parent feel better about themselves and their life – would have left you longing, in vain, for an actual loving connection, for a mirror that might reflect back who you really are.

Until now that is…

Part 2

Moving Towards Balanced Connection

CHAPTER 4

What Do You Do About It?

I've explained why your brain, with its negativity and confirmation biases, is naturally inclined to threat/reward, sticking to, and making bigger, all the bad stuff and letting all the good, or just non-threatening, stuff drift on past you. We've seen that, without deliberate management, your natural experience over time will often be to find/imagine the flaws in, and therefore **to turn against**, whatever and whoever you're looking at. Other than when you're in that initial, involuntary, 'falling in love' with someone state, it's often harder for you to love (connect) than it is to hate (disconnect). And then your brain looks for quick fixes to feel better. It's pretty clear that your brain just isn't naturally designed for sustained well-being and contentment, but to let threat/reward dominate and cause you problems instead.

I believe much of this is thankfully avoidable and I will explain in Part 3 how you can change your experience by **intentionally and consciously work towards building and staying in connection and keeping yourself in balance**.

You may not be keen on the idea of common solutions to common problems, because we all seem so different. Our diversity is, of course, one of our beauties. But this isn't about you living a cookie-cutter life or being a cookie-cutter person. You can be as different and complex as your vast imagination permits. Living with dominant threat means you've been using your imagination to procrastinate, excessively worry, ruminate, overcomplicate and take apart just about anything and anyone though. And, when you're controlled by reward, your imagination is often just taken up with meeting your need for fun and pleasure. In contrast, as you'll see in Principle 6, you'll need to use your creative imagination to put you into, and keep you in, connection.

There are common ways that people get caught in threat/reward and therefore common paths through, although with different ingredients added to suit individual tastes. In fact, real-ising how similar we all are, and that these struggles are present within **all** of us (no matter what we look like from the outside), of itself will connect you with others. Once you know these connecting basics and have moved more firmly into connection, you can build your uniqueness from there.

You need to be sure that the person that you are is actually who you want/are truly meant to be, rather than because something was lacking in your early experience. You need to be able to distinguish being controlled by threat/reward – your wound – from your genuine needs. Is your high sex drive actually dominant reward? Do you do so many things because you're energetic and productive, or are you trying to escape from threat? Is your wanderlust driven by excitement and interest in the world, or do you go to so many places because you believe the grass is always greener and threat always finds the problem with where you are now? Is your introversion really a result of too much threat? Is your extroversion really excessive threat causing you to lack trust in your own decision-making abilities and making 'alone time' uncomfortable? Perhaps your choice of partner is rooted in a need for safety and reward only, rather than real connection and love. Maybe you want to live/work alone because dominant threat makes people 'hell' for you. Is your constant competitiveness a sign that you are controlled by reward? Maybe, rather than not being good at, or wanting, long-term relationships, you're actually sex addicted.

You may now be conscious of the fact that you've been occupying threat/reward too often and this can be a helpful breakthrough in itself. To actually move more into connection though, you need to practise connection (in thoughts, feelings/body and behaviours, as I explain in Principle 4) so much that it crowds threat/reward out, eventually becoming the new default way you relate to self and others. As you know now, because of your brain structure, much of the connection you want to experience, apart from the involuntary falling in love, is going to be the connection you **actively make**. Threat/reward will auto-matically survive and thrive where you forget to do this, so try to consciously do it now whenever you can.

As important as knowing how to recognise threat/reward and turn them down, much of your effort therefore needs to go into turning connection up. The principles I've set out in Part 3 largely focus on doing this. Remember, whatever you give your attention to grows (as neuropsychologist Donald Hebb says 'neurons that fire together, wire together'), if you spend too much time looking at threat/reward like they're the enemy, you'll carry on gluing yourself to them. Remember, you can only be in either threat or connection at any one time, so, while your attention is on these connection-dominated principles, you're out of threat/reward and into where you want to be.

As you resource yourself with more connection, threat/reward will just be made aware that, although they served a helpful purpose long ago, they're not needed as much now and that a life in balanced connection really is the best way to take care of yourself and others from now on.

CHAPTER 5

Managing Change

As you look to move from being controlled by threat/reward to living in balanced connection, it's helpful to hold in mind some important points about change.

It's Possible

You **can** change and, in fact, things **must** change. Change **is** life – it's inevitable. However hard you've fallen, whatever the emotional injury, whatever you've done, or not done, for however long, you've never fallen so far, or so hard, that you can't move more into balanced connection from this day on. It's never too late. You're **always** able; you just need to be willing.

When threat tells you you're hopeless and helpless and that your distress is permanent, you need to consciously and compassionately undo these thought knots. Of course, the deeper the wound and the longer it's been there, the more deeply engrained threat/reward can be. But your incredible brain is always plastic. If your existing neural pathways stayed this way forever, you'd never experience neurological change as you age. Think of all you've learned to do and be over the years. At birth, you couldn't speak, play a sport, do maths. And yet now you can do these complicated things often without even thinking about them.

It's just that now, you're taking more responsibility for, and control of, your neurological change. And you're in far greater control of this than outward-in threat leads you to believe.

And It's Hard

As much as change is inevitable, controlling it is often hard. If you don't accept this, threat/reward can use your struggle as another stick to beat you with.

You've seen in Chapter 2 why threat/reward becomes deep-rooted and powerful early on. Without awareness and trying to change, you'll naturally deal with situations in the future as you have done in the past and view the future based on the past – you'll repeat patterns. We've evolved to do this. How can you get out of bed with any kind of certainty each day if you don't assume, without thinking, that there will be a floor to meet your feet? That 'the best predictor of your future behaviour is past behaviour' is a great survival and success skill when it's a healthy, creative habit, but not when it's based on dominant threat/reward. From threat's point of view, as long as you make it through the day alive and have reward for a smattering of highs, its job is done. But this is really only a partially lived life.

You need to relate to yourself with compassion, under-standing, empathy, patience, humour, trust and forgiveness – all connection qualities – when you're finding change difficult. Holding in mind what you now know about brain development and your biases should help with this. This will, in turn, provide the environment necessary within you to make the changes you want more easily. More on this in Principle 3 (page 83).

So It Takes Time

Your move from threat to balanced connection isn't a three-week process. You'll often be **changing habits of a lifetime**. Some changes can be noticeable straight away, such as having more distance from your threat thoughts, but others, like communicating your anger more helpfully, can be gradual, a process of trial and error over months and even years. **And that's okay because you have years.**

You may not even be consciously aware of changes happening for a time. Maybe the butterflies in your stomach just aren't there as much. I know people who realised after a few months that their nails looked longer, which meant they'd been biting them less – and that's how they knew they were feeling safer. Of course, big shifts and insights can happen in a split second, but after light bulb moments and epiphanies, the realisations need to be worked into everyday life. This takes time, patience and gentle, persistent awareness.

It's worth holding in mind that patience isn't **that** you wait, it's **how** you wait; you need to try to wait **calmly**. Impatience, because it means you're annoyed, can of itself be a dominant threat/reward quality. It's inevitable that as you go on you'll slip back into threat/reward ways – that's part of the process. It's therefore important to ground changes where you can as you go along by writing them down. Some people like to keep a handwritten journal of progress, spending 10 minutes or so in the morning setting their intentions for the day and the same time in the evening reflecting on progress and/or any reasons to be grateful for the day (see page 87 on the significance of gratitude). Bear in mind that spending your time **taking stock** and grounding how far you've come is connection behaviour.

Remember, your external environment and many of your relationships may currently set up in a way that knows and supports you living largely in threat/reward. Important aspects of your emotional development might have slowed down at the time these traits became dominant. Imagine a 45-year-old who began to use weed or pornography as a 13-year-old to manage threat. Once he stops doing it, he has to learn to face adult life with a limited emotional toolkit. His threat feelings can't be managed and/or aliveness felt any more using just on-demand dopamine shots. He's going to need to rebuild relationships with himself and others with courage, based on sober trust and intimacy, instead of the connection mimicked by being stoned or post-coitus.

As you make this journey, you'll replace much of the, at times, lonely, annoying and/or scary world that too much threat/reward has made for you with more sustaining and nurturing connection, until it builds enough mass to leave being controlled by threat/reward in your past. You may find the move to this 'new normal' of balanced connection difficult, so be patient with yourself. I've heard it said that a problem takes as long to leave life as it took to become a part of it. This is a daunting prospect if you're looking at roots in childhood experience. I think it's an exaggeration with what we now know about psychology and neurology, but do hold it in mind when threat turns on you for doing the thing you hoped you wouldn't do again; when you unconsciously, or even consciously, let threat/reward control you again. This isn't a linear process and your neural pathways don't just disappear overnight – you need to know the balanced connection alternatives and to reinforce them through behaviour change over time.

Something else to bear in mind is that, no matter how distressing the life you're currently 'living' seems to be, you might be getting some, albeit hidden, benefit from living it this way. A benefit that, therefore, quietly encourages and sustains a life dominated by threat/reward. Anxiety and depression, for example, can mean you're looked after by others more than you would otherwise be in life. They might mean you can have the rights of adulthood without some of its responsibilities. In most cases though, rather than an addiction to the threat/reward drama being a lifestyle choice, I just think it's really hard to break lifelong patterns and to know what to do instead.

It's a Journey

Related to patience, you'll be on spectrums in your use of threat, reward and connection and will have moved along them over time. To start and continue with balanced connection I'm suggesting you're going to need to take control of their dials and see, through experience, where balance sits for you and how to maintain it throughout your life. Over time it'll be much easier to stay in balance as the changes you make bear fruit.

However, although your quality of life will improve with balanced connection, often profoundly, it doesn't mean trying to be some 'perfect' person or live in a 'perfect world'. Perfection is all in threat's mind – there's no such thing. In fact, you'll see that when you let go of the need for perfection, of threat always looking to some point in the future when everything will be great at last (which it'll never actually allow you to find), your life in **this moment** will often feel more than enough, just as it is. I talk more about the power of this moment in Principle 5 (page 127).

'If Nothing Changes, Nothing Changes' (writer, Earnie Larsen)

When dictated by threat you might have a tendency to engage in 'shelf development' – lots of reading about psychology and high-level concepts, while behavioural patterns largely stay the same. Sometimes this reading can actually be used to feed threat's compensating specialness and grandiosity. Threat and reward produce all kinds of denial and reasons to continue with them and have access to all of your trillion neurons to do this.

Some of the most important changes in the move from threat/reward domination to balanced connection might 'just' be about how you experience yourself and others, but it's likely your **behaviours** will be different as you change. It's a coaching principle that you are what you do: 'as is your deed, so is your destiny' (Upanishads). Although this is an oversimplification, it's true that, even with cognitive insight, nothing changes if nothing changes. You therefore need to be open to actually **doing things differently**. It's not enough just to wish for better and go on doing the same thing. You need to try to **make** it better, by behaviour change, as I explain in Principle 4 (page 93).

Only Change Because You Want To

It's important that you're making these changes because that's the best way to take care of yourself from this point on – ideally change needs to come from a place of connection to yourself. If your motivation is a belief of inadequacy, that there's something fundamentally wrong with you, this is being motivated by threat.

Try to believe, at least in theory, that you're not making the changes suggested in this book because you're defective as you are, but, instead, that they're necessary acts of self-care that you deserve now. I talk more about improving your loving connection to yourself throughout all of the 10 principles.

Fake It to Make It

Most of the energy you experience is actually emotional energy and, as you know, we want your emotional motivators in the future to come more from connection. The difficulty is that when threat or reward dominate you'll have limited access to them. You'll mainly do things, or stop doing things, because of threat feelings and/or reward. Until you start to produce connection feelings more naturally, you may need to begin the new connection behaviours I talk about in Principles 4 and 7 without necessarily feeling like you want to. For the time being at least, you're sometimes going to need to **fake it to make it**. By doing this, over time, you'll get rewarded by the new connection behaviours which will build up momentum in your changes.

Be Brave

As you'd expect, threat makes new behaviours and people frightening. Susan Jeffers's '**Feel the fear and do it anyway**' can be a new mantra for you. You know threat's below-the-radar belief is that change – the unknown – will kill you. It won't, so take some deep breaths and try to go ahead when you can in spite of these messages.

Accept What You Can't Change and Change What You Can

There are some important ideas in the Serenity Prayer of the AA's 12-Step Programme. Written with addicts in mind, it works as well for threat as it does for reward. The principles are that you need to:

1. Stay calm, so you can accept and let go of the things you're unable to change.
2. Be brave enough to change the things you're able to.
3. Try to know the difference between points 1. and 2.

I think this is a helpful filter for all your experience. If you have a problem, can you do anything about it? Yes? Then go ahead and try to do whatever is needed. If the answer's no, then let go of the issue and try to focus your attention elsewhere. I'll look specifically at managing attention in Principle 5 (page 127).

As you know, threat will always be pushing your attention outwards, for example getting annoyed about other people's behaviour, when that's actually not something that's within your control. The only thing that is within your control is **your** response to it. It will also mean you might lack the courage to, for example, be honest with yourself and others in a way that would change your life for the better. You're going to need to be mindful of how threat might be working in this way at the moment. I talk about this more in Principle 1 (page 69).

Seemingly Small Changes Can Have Great Consequences

Threat's feast, or famine, tendency might mean you believe changes must be dramatic to be worth anything. But there are so many ways to make the move to balanced connection, whether through thoughts, feelings, body, behaviour, people and the things around you. Although going from being controlled by threat/reward to balanced connection can be a huge shift, it's most often done in small steps in your moment-by-moment experience of life: a cup filled drop by drop.

You can build momentum over time in lots of little ways: a small change to your daily routine, not getting so angry at yourself if you stub your toe, catching a threat/reward thought and letting it go rather than riding it, flossing your teeth more often, drinking one more glass of water a day, sleeping 15 minutes longer a day or sending a thoughtful text to a friend. These are all pulled threads in the excessive threat/reward blanket and it'll over time unravel to reveal connection.

A change in one area will often mean changes in others. Compartmentalising your experience is an illusion. Your work life doesn't exist in isolation to your relationships. It's all you. When you take better care of yourself around an abusive partner, you'll find it easier to resist that chocolate box; when you resist the chocolates, you'll feel more relaxed in a pressurised meeting. And the more relaxed you feel, the more you'll be able to start imagining and working more towards the future you want.

As I've said above, it's important to keep a note of all the changes you're making, large and small, to ground them, so that when threat/reward try to tell you you're 'back to square one', it's hopeless and you may as well not bother, you can gently, but firmly, show yourself this just isn't true.

Prioritise

Because it only sees problems, too much threat can produce a paralysing, overwhelming list of things you need to do and stop doing. Try to **prioritise** on the basis of what's most important to you and write this down. It can be helpful to have stage one and two changes; stage one being something you're doing differently today, or this week, with stage two including the changes to threat/reward beliefs and values you're always working towards as the foundations of a more balanced connection life (see Principle 4).

Say It in the Positive

When you decide what it is you want to change, your goal or value shouldn't be said in the negative, i.e. 'I don't want to (x) anymore.' Just identifying problems, or 'lack of', is living in threat/reward. You therefore need to think about what it is you **want and need** instead, i.e. the balanced connection alternative. Instead of thinking 'I don't want to get so easily annoyed with myself and other people', try to frame it in terms of 'I'm patient with myself and others.' Think 'I want a loving partner', rather than 'I don't want to be on my own anymore.'

Now's the Time

Related to the fact that nothing changes if nothing changes, it's important to begin **now**. As the Dalai Lama said: 'there are only two days of the year that nothing can be done. One is called yesterday and the other is called tomorrow.' You can start over in any moment and, as Tara Brach suggests, 'how you live **today** is how you live your life', because that's all that's real. The longer you have a wound, the more time threat/reward have to take root in every part of your life. Try to be open to life being different in some way today and actively think of how that might be. And, yes, even having these thoughts count, because they're connection thoughts of hope.

Accept It's Probably Going to Hurt

You'll find that some psychological aspects of you will need to break down, so that you can build up new connection alternatives. Some of this break down will feel freeing and enjoyable, while others might hurt; if, for example, you decide you're no longer going to be dependent on a partner or friend, psychologically or otherwise, it could mean the end of the relationship and therefore an experience of loss for you. But feeling hurt is a part of life. Allow yourself to feel it and it will pass like everything else.

Always Remember It's Worth It

The fact you only know what you know can stand in the way of your move to balanced connection. The unknown can be frightening when you're living in balanced connection, let alone if threat/reward dominate. I understand you might be taking risks here without knowing how good it's going to feel on the other side. However, try to hold in mind both the benefits of making this journey and also what could be at stake if you don't.

In terms of what's at stake if you carry on as you are, try to imagine your life in three years' time if you don't make any changes. Use your fear to your advantage here. Depending on what your experience of life is like now, this picture can be a big motivator for change. For example, if you're addicted to gambling, just imagine what your relationships with yourself and other people will be like if you carry on in this way for another few years: more shame, more debt, the loss of respect of friends and family, the continuation of secrets and lies and suicidal thoughts. Imagine what all of this will really **feel** like. And what if you continue to allow threat to dominate, as your world progressively narrows, friends fall away and you remain angrily stuck in jobs, places and relationships that you mostly don't enjoy and have little hope of changing? Then imagine in as much detail as you can what life might be like if you took those important steps to a more connected life. What might your world look and feel like if you moved the addiction out of your life? What would life be like if you saw the world as a place of limitless possibilities and opportunities, rather than something to defend against? I talk about this again in Principle 6 (page 137).

If your life, although at times distressing, is often 'fine', I want you to try to hold on to the belief that, in balanced connection, you'll feel more alive, purposeful, accepted and content with a clearer idea of who you are, how you've got here and where you're going. You'll be enough for yourself. Try to **keep the faith, never give up and always trust** the process.

Part 3

The 10 Principles

The following 10 principles outline ways in which you can move from being controlled by threat/reward to living in balanced connection, mainly by working on connection. Maybe keep a list of these suggestions: let them play on your mind; add to and/or adapt them, as long as you're trying to think of a way forward. If you don't believe one will work for you, then decide (and try to decide, not procrastinate over) what you'll do instead.

You need to make sure you're not just stopping at reasons why not; that's threat taking apart, designing cul de sacs and throwing problems into the air that don't land in resolutions. Threat already knows what you don't like and don't want and need, **I want to know what you like, want and need** instead. When you're in balanced connection, you decide if something isn't for you, usually after trying it a couple of times, and then imagine another possibility.

1 Take
RESPONSIBILITY

CHAPTER 6

Principle 1: Take Responsibility

A key way to shift from being controlled by threat/reward to living in balanced connection is to make sure you're taking full responsibility for your experience, including the consequences of your behaviour. As we've seen, because threat/reward are persistently outward-focused, you might have a tendency to noodle around other people's behaviour with mild outrage. And, of course, other people dominated by threat/reward will often give your threat biases plenty to chew over.

Try to hold in mind that threat's preoccupation with other people is mostly in vain. Understandably, threat wants you to change the things it's frightened/angry about, but you're unable to **consistently control** another adult's behaviour – that's really an impossible task. As you know, loving someone can have a profound effect on them and therefore their behaviour, moving them into connection, but if they're not actively doing the work themselves to remain in connection at other times, this is unlikely to last. You can then only control your response to them. **Some of the most important freedoms you have in life are the freedoms to control your response, to change your mind and to take care of your own business.** And, as you can't take care of your own and another person's business at the same time, this may often involve, for your own self-care, **minding your own business**.

Of course, if you change the way you behave towards others that'll shift the relationship dynamic. If you spend more time in connection, you'll be more loving towards yourself and others, resulting in others feeling more loved and this will usually then be paid back and forth between you. But you need to try to see this as a by-product; you're not making these changes to change, or help, another. This begins and ends with you.

While threat has been too dominant, you may not have been looking inside long enough to look at your part in a problem.

Threat's black-and-white, victim–perpetrator format looks for someone to blame, someone at fault, rather than necessarily for you to take some responsibility. Threat thoughts want you to be angry at someone, either internally or externally, firmly believing there's some kind of objective truth when it comes to humans. Most often threat will tell you you're the victim, that it's unfair and the other person is to 'blame'. And the anger that results means you might flip between victim and perpetrator. Threat often ignores the fact that it takes two to love, two to argue, two to both begin and keep a healthy, or unhealthy, dynamic going. That often maybe neither of you are 'right' and neither of you are 'wrong'.

Threat language includes:

'Well he/she won't do this, so why should I?'

This is the place of tit for tat, victim/perpetrator and the frustrating illusions of trapped and stalemate.

'He/she made me angry/feel small/feel like shit/cry/hit him/her'

It's fine if someone makes you laugh, inspires you or turns you on (all connection/helpful reward experiences), but the outward-in, victim, 'done to' position implicit in the phrase 'made me' takes your experience out of your psychological control and therefore, riskily, outside of your choice.

Similar to 'made' you, do it/think it/feel it are also saying that others drag you down, wear you out, put you through, wind you up, do your head in, let you down, put you in a mood, piss you off, drive you mad, get inside your head, stress you out and annoy/outrage/bore/upset you. To move more into balanced connection, try to hold in mind that no one can **make you** feel anything: other people shouldn't have control over your thoughts and feelings/body in the way this implies. It's helpful to think less in terms of you 'couldn't help' yourself and more in terms of having made a choice to do it, for whatever reason.

For example, it's not a place of connection with self and others to say you cheated on your partner because they didn't 'make' you feel good enough about yourself. In balanced connection, that wouldn't be all their responsibility anyway. Of course, you're always doing your best and I really do understand why we can see an affair with someone else as the only way of temporarily helping ourselves to feel better. At least theoretically though, you need to accept that, from a self-care point of view, you had other, more preferable, options such as relationship counselling, if things weren't going well. It can be threat-controlled unhelpful (for you) blaming behaviour and avoiding taking personal responsibility to suggest otherwise.

You'd clearly struggle not to be shocked or annoyed if someone hit you. But, aside from such extreme situations, try not to remain for long in the place of being a victim or 'done to' in your own mind. Be conscious that you can be the agent of your own thoughts and feelings. To move further into balanced connection, you need to hold in mind now that **your response is your choice**. This choice is, of course, understandably much less clear in the case of addictions and compulsions, but, even with them, over time I hope you'll experience more choice as you work through these principles.

You might also need to curb the tendency to say sorry to another person for 'making' them feel a particular way, because you didn't. You'll only apologise for what you did, or didn't do, if and when your internal connection guide, which I talk about in detail in Principle 5, agrees you should, bearing in mind the other person's view. You're not magical enough to 'make' others feel something and vice versa.

'I can't'

To increase connection with yourself, try to watch the use of the word 'can't'. Maybe replace it with 'won't' and see how that changes things. You'll have lots of imagined 'cant's' when threat dominates because of the trapped/victim complex, but few are real. It's important to remember you **always have a choice**. 'Can't' is most often an imagined barrier to change that means you may not try to understand why you're doing or not doing something and might avoid taking control and responsibility as a result. It's not that you 'can't' retrain at your age, or say no to going to your parents' for Christmas, or say sorry, or tell someone you love them; it's that you **won't**. Sometimes, of course, you won't for helpful reasons. In threat, understandably, the reason will often be because you're frightened/angry. In balanced connection, it's helpful to admit this to yourself, try to move into connection and see if it changes things for you.

I'm 'lucky'

If you use this word to say you're grateful, it's connection. But if grateful, or thankful, is what you actually mean, you could say that. If you're saying you have what you have because you're lucky in the sense of some external, superstitious influence, that could be threat speaking. It can suggest a lack of ownership – the presence of some uncontrollable, random power at work governing your life. Threat won't allow you to take responsibility for the good things that happen because of **who and what you are**, because it just doesn't see them.

In balanced connection, you'll need to try to own and take responsibility, not just for the troubling experiences you might have a part in, but also the good ones. Life isn't all a lucky dip or lottery. You haven't just been 'lucky' in achieving what you have. More likely you're good at what you do and have a range of skills and qualities that mean you can function well in life at times. You need to be conscious of threat's biases and 'imposter syndrome'.

In balanced connection, you know it won't all collapse if you say well done to yourself for the good things you do, or even the bad things you don't do, not because you're 'lucky', but because of who you are as a person. Try to list in your mind, or on paper, all the qualities that have enabled you to do this (see page 103 for more on this). This will connect you more to the solid foundations you're already standing on to navigate life even without changing anything.

The other side of the threat coin here is that things haven't always gone the way you'd like because you're 'unlucky'. Try to be curious about how many of your current difficulties are a result of being controlled by threat/reward. If you decide some are, calmly own this and look into what you're going to do about it now. You can think about the skills and qualities you might need to develop more of to resolve your difficulties from this point, along with any threat/reward aspects of personality to be managed out over time.

In short, in balanced connection, you won't let good, or bad, 'luck' be an abrogation of your personal responsibility. You decide your destiny and your fate now. You know you're not responsible for **anything** that happened to you as a child, but, as an adult, you own and navigate your life and, calmly and gently, can take full responsibility for yourself and your behaviour.

When threat is too dominant, you might also:

- Frequently use the word 'you' when you mean 'I'. Maybe this is because of threat's external focus, or its struggle to own your experience, or because, in threat, you often only really exist psychologically when you think others are looking at you. If you're talking about your experiences, beliefs, opinions and/ or values, then it's important to own them from this point: so try saying 'I' instead of 'you' and see how different it feels.

- Worry about what's 'normal' and say 'doesn't everyone do that?' Because it's preoccupied with trying to keep you safe, threat often worries about whether the things you're thinking, feeling or doing are 'normal' or 'weird'. Not the place for colours, even shades of grey, threat needs black or white, good or bad, normal or weirdo. It believes not being 'normal' threatens your survival and will therefore stop you walking outside of some, often completely imagined, boundary. I look more at this in Principle 4 (page 93). In balanced connection, try to be aware that most of the time now these are pretty wasted worries.

- Pepper sentences with 'kind of', 'sort of' or 'I guess' and often end them with 'I don't know'. These expressions of doubt, confusion and vagueness potentially show how threat compromises your internal connection, particularly feelings/ the body, as we'll see in Principle 4 (page 93).

- Be reluctant to call yourself a 'man' or 'woman', any gender identity issues aside here. You might use 'boy' or 'girl' instead. Maybe it shows on some level you're aware how threat/

reward can compromise aspects of emotional development, or maybe threat is putting you down or avoiding taking responsibility. In balanced connection, you need to hold in mind that you, and all the adults around you, are **men or women** now.

Why does threat, when it's not blaming you, blame others rather than take responsibility in a balanced way? As well as threat's anger and outward-in perspective, it can also be less painful to look at the unhelpful ways other people operate, instead of your own. Cogitating about others' flaws can also feed threat's compensating superiority. Judging them is a way of feeling better about yourself in a 'Wow, they're crazy, I would never do that' type of way. Although you might have done that, you're just not often spending enough time looking at your own behaviour to notice. Or you're not doing it right at this moment.

There's a concept in therapy of 'shadow', which means splitting disliked parts of your personality off from your own awareness and recognising and criticising them in other people, commonly, for example, selfishness, being judgemental or bullying behaviour. For a more balanced connection, try to be curious about whether someone else is actually a mirror of parts of yourself that threat might often be hiding from you.

In the Beginning...

Another reason you might not be used to always taking personal responsibility is that you spent your early years understandably having no responsibility for anything. Someone else decided what you ate and wore, where you went, what was dangerous, safe, good, bad or indifferent. Control over your life largely sat outside of you. With caregivers dominated by threat, even if you were given the luxury of showing you were distressed or angry, nothing much may have changed as a result. You were probably told it was bad behaviour to want to decide for yourself. As we've seen, threat caregivers often view difference in their children (aka little extensions of themselves) as threatening to them.

As we saw in Chapter 2, when your brain was at its most impressionable, you may have got into the habit of disliking yourself and living with things you were unhappy about. And being impotently angry about it. You internalised the belief that it's naughty or selfish to want to be different. If you were a 'good' child, you largely complied with caregivers' wishes. If you were a 'naughty' child, you often disobeyed them. Either way, whether through attachment to, or fear of, them, you may have got used to orbiting with passive, or expressed, anger around threat/reward caregivers, possibly leading to you doing the same as an adult in relation to your parents/a partner/friends/a boss. You need to be curious about whether, without knowing it, you're making yourself and/or others pay in relationships today for a lack of connection in your early experience.

Try to hold in mind now that whatever your caregivers might have done that was unhelpful for you, was about their own limitations and not you. You really were 'made' like this. However, as a balanced, connected adult, you know to replace threat words like blame or fault, with responsibility. Rather than ask, 'Why does she treat me like this?', in balanced connection you might now ask, 'How do I contribute to the dynamic?', 'Why do I collude with it?' How are you going to make it different by changing an aspect of how you relate? Or should you leave the relationship?

Always Look Inside First

In balanced connection, you need to notice physiologically when you're triggered with threat feelings and go inwards to look at what's happening for you. Try to give yourself some time and space to look at what's going on inside you and to decide on a conscious response rather than reacting. When anger or fear push your attention outwards, try to get curious about what's happening inside you. Think in terms of **'dropping inside'** your internal world, not to look for a victim, but with connected curiosity, patience and empathy, firstly for yourself and then for the other. What's underneath your distress? What's threat making this mean? What stories is threat telling you about the other person? Are you going to choose to do something about it? Is it best taking care of you/others to do so?

In any difficult situation, you can:

1. Choose to accept how it is.
2. Try to change it (bearing in mind that you can't change another adult).

3.   Leave the situation.

One of the greatest payoffs for taking responsibility is that, if you know you're choosing this life and why, there's less feeling angry towards an imagined 'they' about how unfair aspects of it might be. Because you know it's your decision. In balanced connection, you'll feel angry and then take responsibility for doing something to change it where you can. If you can't change it, you'll accept it. This is freeing, relieving and empowering.

It's your version of events and your life now. If you want to paint it black, you can. You can, of course, choose to tolerate a difficult relationship, but try to consciously know why, acknowledge the cost to you and be aware it's a choice. If you carry on doing things you don't want to do, that's your responsibility now. Just like if you're going to feel mostly happy, fulfilled and content in life, it's because you choose to.

Choice can be frightening to realise:

•   What are you really capable of in this life if you stop avoiding through fear and actually go towards it?

•   How do you deal compassionately and empathetically with the fact that, today, it's your responsibility to fulfil your potential?

•   What is your full connection potential?

•   What are your balanced, connected values, opinions and beliefs outside of the threat/reward ones given to you by previous generations (we'll look further at this in Principle 4)?

•   What will 'the new normal' you're developing be like?

As you move from being controlled by threat/reward to living in balanced connection, maybe hold in mind Gandhi's words: be the change that you wish to see in the world. No one's going to consistently save you, protect you or change you, except you. People can, and will, help you in many ways (see Principle 8), but try to hold in mind that **it isn't someone else's responsibility to do it for you, or to you**. That's not even possible. And, thankfully, as you'll see, you can save, protect, change and make yourself happy, in spite of what dominant threat/reward may want you to believe.

Of course, because change is hard and threat looks outwards, you'll often initially look out to others to make changes, for example, therapists (see Principle 5), coaches, spiritual traditions, gurus and all different types of 'experts', advisers, self-development books and courses. Threat will compare your internal experience, which may at times have been chaotic, with the seeming external calm of another and believe they have the answers. You'll have bought this book presumably on the basis that I might be able to tell you something helpful that you didn't already know. And I'm glad you did. Again, it's a balance here. You may not be able to make this journey on your own in the early stages. If you could have done that, you would have. Going to others for help makes good, balanced connection, sense. At the very least, it's based on connected hope and trust of others. People can and will help you on this journey, and more healthy, intimate relationships with others are certainly one of the main ways to balanced connection, as we'll see in Principle 8.

Ultimately, though, you need to take responsibility for yourself and building and maintaining balanced connection over time. When threat gives over too much power to other people, you're open to manipulation and even to becoming an actual victim. Threat may often have been an unhelpful internal guide, but you need to believe that you have the potential for the same wisdom as any other person you project this onto. You might just need some help with accessing and putting lots of connected thought, feeling and behavioural energy into your own guide (see Principle 5). Any help you get from others, including therapy, shouldn't be forever continuing the belief that the best judge of your future path is **outside** of you.

You might also hold in mind that balanced connection is **only** about taking responsibility for yourself and any dependents, such as children or pets. It doesn't include other adults. Giving advice to, loving, supporting and even staging 'interventions' with others can be connecting behaviours, but threat might overestimate what you can actually do to change another adult's psychological state. Your partner and parents are not your dependents in balanced connection. Balanced, connected love between adults is not about dependency. Rescuing others can be part of threat's victim/perpetrator/rescuer drama triangle. Taking too much responsibility for other adults when they really should be looking after themselves, and when you really should be looking after yourself, is potentially threat co-dependency and too much care-taking. Try not to give that as much of your attention from now on.

loyalty
trust
patience
honesty
passion
gratitude
kindness
compassion
acceptance
integrity
intimacy
forgiveness
empathy
humour
courage
warmth

2 Decide on your
MEANING OF LOVE

CHAPTER 7

Principle 2: Decide on Your Meaning Of Love

Connection is the solid foundation you're now working to build and stand more on. The most common connecting word you use and hear is probably 'love'. However, your meaning of love may have been formed through a largely threat/reward lens, so you need to take a fresh look at it now.

You've seen that caregivers controlled by threat/reward will have modelled a confusing account of love. Some fear/anger-based controlling, even abusive, behaviour might have been followed by 'You know I only do it because I love you/care so much.' Narcissistic caregivers no doubt believe they're loving their child as they compromise its emotional development with 'special' treatment. Excessive threat will often confuse its control, martyrdom, anger, jealousy and enmeshment with love because that's as much as it can really do and is all it's ever known. You may have received little in the way of **real**, connected love in the past and therefore you may struggle to do something that hasn't been shown to you.

When threat is too dominant, you might believe the angrier someone gets with you, or you get with them, or the more you try to control each other, the more 'love' must surely be present. Threat might even say you love someone, but you don't like them. Well, I think love (connection) and dislike (disconnection) are **mutually exclusive states at any one time**. And if you get more angry with a person than you do with anybody else in your life, the relationship may actually be characterised by threat, which is light years away from being in love with that person.

An extreme example of this is smacking a child and saying that it's out of love/care. When you calmly, clearly and cleanly express boundaries to take care of a child's well-being, that's balanced connection love. Putting your hands on any other person, particularly a dependent, defenceless one, a third of your size, whose well-being you volunteered to be responsible for, is just not managing anger well enough. If you put your hands on another person in anger, you've lost control. And children follow your example, not advice. It's important not to let threat dress physical abuse up as loving, unless you want your children to tolerate and/or perpetrate violence themselves. Looking at physical violence generally, girls who see their mothers get hit, are considerably more likely to get hit themselves in relationships. Boys who see their mothers get hit, are more likely to hit their partners. And just to make it clear that this is a human issue rather than just a male one, it's believed that in a significant proportion of domestic violence situations involving men and women, it's actually the woman who puts her hands on the man first.

If your fantasy of being with a person is better than the reality, if you have your most loving thoughts and feelings about your partner when you're away on a business trip, then try to be curious about what you understand love/loving behaviour to be. As a simple rule, as writer Chuck Spezzano says, **'if it hurts, it isn't love'**.

The first theory taught on therapy courses is often the 'person-centred therapy' of Carl Rogers. He suggests that people will actually self-regulate when three qualities are present. These are that the therapist must:

1. be completely genuine;
2. have unconditional positive regard for their client; and
3. strive to show empathy for their client.

Maybe what Rogers is describing here are some of the foundations and qualities of a balanced connection loving relationship.

For Rogers, it might have been honesty, empathy for, and unconditional acceptance of, another. But what is your **vision** of the word love now? Bearing in mind, as Stephen R Covey suggests, that **'love is a verb'**, a **doing** word. 'You should know I love you, or I wouldn't be with you' is potentially young child/ parent territory.

It's helpful to make a list of what you believe to be loving qualities in order to ground your concept of love. These might include: loyalty, trust, patience, honesty, acceptance, respect, sensitivity, passion, gratitude, compassion, equanimity, integrity, forgiveness, kindness, support, intimacy, commitment, humour, openness, spaciousness, empathy, courage, contentment, encouragement, freedom, fun, warmth, curiosity, care, etc. How many of these **characterised** the 'love' you were shown as a child? Maybe not many, but you now get to decide what love means in your life.

We'll look at a number of these loving qualities in more detail in Principle 3 in the context of self-love. It's important you hold in mind that your relationship with self is **always** the place to start before you can go out with any change. When threat dominates, you can struggle so much to connect with love internally that you keep going out to others for it, i.e. potentially love addiction and/or co-dependency. You might talk about **going out and finding** love as a way to help you to feel better. However, when you fall in love with someone, you've actually just been able to connect to the love (connection) part of yourself. You're therefore as much in love with yourself as the other person.

Try to hold in mind that people don't give love to you; they look, behave, sound, smell and taste in a way that triggers your own connection part. And because they don't actually give it to you, they can't take it away. Connection is always accessible within you; it's just waiting there, patiently, for you to connect with it. As you connect with it more, you'll likely find some sadness there at first, as we'll see in Principle 4, but, after you feel that sadness as much as you need to, you'll move through it to a more settled balanced connection that integrates, in its largest part, a healthy and energetic love both of self and others.

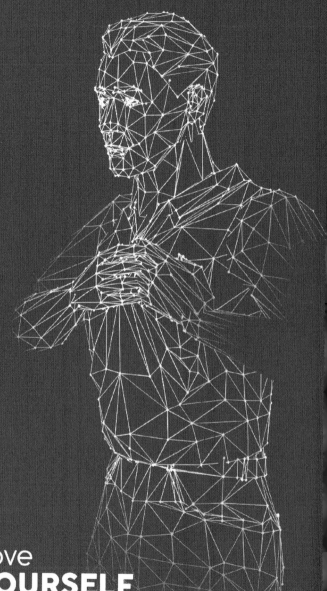

3 Love
YOURSELF

CHAPTER 8

Principle 3: Love Yourself

When threat/reward dominate, you have to go out to find love. In balanced connection you know that a loving relationship with yourself is the place to start. **You find love right where you are.** You'll need to take your new definition of love and look first at whether, more often than not, you're behaving lovingly towards yourself. When you relate to self with love, it naturally flows out to others and they'll often feel more loving towards you as a result.

I believe that when you say the kind of loving things to yourself that you'd like others to be saying to you, it has a similar calming, connecting effect internally as someone else saying them to you. The same applies when you say loving things **to** others. Whoever you're hearing it from – whether it's you saying it to someone else, someone else saying it to you or, in this case, you saying it to you – you're still hearing it; you're still in a place of connection with self and others. Of course this isn't intended to mean you won't need and want others to behave in a loving way towards you, because you always will. It's just we don't want your sense of loving and being loved to be **entirely dependent** on others, who aren't always going to be in a place to provide the love you want and need.

Compassion

In the same way as you look outwards through a problem-finding lens when threat controls you, you'll also be looking inwards through it. Most of the worst things you hear said about yourself will probably be **inside** your head. It may actually be **you** who often provokes your threat.

Just like in external relationships, too much threat/reward lead to an internal relationship characterised by conflict, polarisation, struggle, one part set against another: true self versus false self; short-term impulsivity versus long-term benefits; the critical parent versus the wounded inner child; connection versus threat/reward. When you're in distress, or have difficulty making changes, your threat anger resolution can be that you 'need a kick up the arse'. This is based on the threat belief that you'll only make changes if you hit yourself hard enough or punish your struggling self. You really won't though. Getting angry at yourself for being angry or frightened is just more of the same. Threat anger actually switches **off** your ability to think clearly and compromises both your capacity to make decisions and to produce the emotional energy we want to motivate you.

You might hear a lot about the value of 'fighting' for things in this life, but in your move from living in threat/reward to balanced connection, you need to try to stop any internal war and accept that you're not going to be able to overcome, excise or exile any part of yourself. You can't kill what you'd like to change without killing yourself, which some people, of course, tragically do in self-hatred/anger. To perceive threat/reward as 'the enemy' – to shame them – is counterproductive; they're as much a part of you as connection, and turning against them just gives them more of your energy. They'll go on living separate lives.

Balanced connection doesn't see threat/reward as weeds in your garden to be hacked down. In fact, your parts are all stronger working **together**. You need to acknowledge and understand why they've developed to dominate in the way that they have and therefore why they now do what they do. Treat them with dignity, because at one point they were just trying to protect you and avoid pain. You're always doing, and always have done, your best, based on your psychological make-up at any given time. Turn towards them with curiosity – they'll lose power the more you listen to their misguided but well-intentioned stories, and then tell them some new balanced connection ones instead.

From this point on, you need to try to relate to dominant threat/reward with loving kindness and concern for self, just as you'd try to behave towards someone you love if they were in similar pain. No one may have consistently cared for you in this way before, but you can now. This won't mean threat/reward continue out of control, it'll actually reduce their energy supply.

And it doesn't mean letting them do whatever they want. You mustn't disown them, but following these principles means you also don't feed them. Compassion isn't an 'anything goes, free rein' response to unhelpful experience. Boundaries are often blurred when threat/reward dominate and establishing and holding them is an important part of this process, as we'll see in Principle 9. But you can take responsibility and know that it's self-care for aspects of you to change without self-blame/hatred.

Connected, compassionate management of threat/reward's thought stream sometimes sounds like just a gentle 'sshh' in your head; at other times, a knowing 'I see you' with permission to pass; and at others, an expansive, calmly expressed, balanced explanation of what's going to happen instead and why. They need to know why they can now relax and hand over the reins more to connection. That a more balanced connection life is actually **safer and more rewarding** without their dominance.

How do you speak to yourself compassionately when you've existed largely in threat/reward for so long? How do you look at yourself with kind eyes now, when no one really did that as you were growing up? I suggest you imagine someone, or something, you'd associate with the quality of loving kindness. It could be a character from a fairy tale, a film, someone who lives down the road, Buddha, Yoda, a colour, an animal – it's up to you. You need to imagine in detail what they'd look, smell and sound like. What they'd be wearing and how they'd move and communicate. The question 'What would Jesus do?' is used as a joke, but you need an equivalent, a quick way to access connection through your imagination. You can then spend time in your imagination with your personification/symbol of connection, relating to it. Giving your attention to something grows it, making it a reliable resource whenever threat/reward want to take control. You need to do the same with the quality of wisdom. It may be, of course, that both compassion and wisdom are qualities of whoever/whatever you choose, which makes it even easier.

Over time, you'll be able to bring this part of you forward in your imagination and communicate with it whenever you need to. As its choices pay off, it'll become an integrated part of you, sinking into your unconscious. This part, your 'guide' as I call it, is explored more in Principle 5.

When you speak to yourself in your head, you might also find it helpful to address yourself in the way you would someone you love. You can reinforce self-compassion by referring to yourself using words such as darling, sweetheart, fella, dear one, good man, my love, buddy… whatever you like. Particularly when threat/reward dominate. Try to be respectful to and go easy on yourself. You need to want you in your life, to give more to yourself than you take and to be there when you need you. No one should love or support you more than you do.

Acceptance

You need to accept yourself as you are, including the things you might want to be different, seeing this move to balanced connection as something you're doing to improve your life. As I mentioned above, it's important not to try to motivate yourself with the belief that you're damaged, shameful or unacceptable as you are.

Integrity

Key to being more in balanced connection is to behave with integrity – to **do the right thing, even when no one's looking**. Threat might tell you to do the right thing, but largely only when others are looking, because when threat dominates that's all that matters and often the only times you really exist. Your integrity behind the scenes can be compromised along the way. You'll need to keep integrity at the forefront of your mind when making behavioural choices now, gradually taking those parts of life and self that nobody else sees back under your control.

Empathy

This is the capacity to put yourself in another's shoes, but needs to include yourself if we're looking at a more connected relationship internally. Try to connect, using your imagination, to what **your** felt experience is and might have been in any given situation, particularly in your early experience. You know what threat might have done in terms of you blaming yourself for distress at the time.

Try to **feel** into the past and present with empathy for yourself, including the frightened and the frightening parts of you and the compulsive and impulsive parts of you. Imagine what it was actually like, based on what you know now, to, for example, live with caregivers like yours, to be bullied or to grow up gay in a heterosexist world. What does it feel like to live in a relationship now that's not going well or do a job you don't enjoy? If having empathy for yourself is difficult at first, because it's so unfamiliar, I suggest you try to imagine someone you really love going through the same distressing things you have/ are. See if this helps you to connect with yourself in the way we need you to here. We'll look generally at threat/reward's difficult relationship with feelings in Principle 4 (page 93).

Gratitude

As you know, threat focuses only on flaws, always looking for the chink in the armour, the Achilles heel. You're therefore going to struggle to recognise all you have to be thankful for. Threat's self-preservation preoccupation is also not the place of heartfelt thank yous. Reward, dominated by craving and yearning for satisfaction, also points you to a lack of in any moment.

Being grateful for where you've been, who you already are and what's around you now is a key way to balanced connection with self and others. **The quickest way to happiness (connection) is to want what you already have.** Gratitude is universally loved and really **a necessity rather than a luxury** from this point on.

If you take your smartphone and press a few buttons to set your recently taken photos to music, it'll move you to connection, by releasing your feel-good chemicals. You need to know how to do this without the use of phone software too, and gratitude is a great way. Having a daily gratitude practice doesn't need to be any more complicated than thinking of three things you're grateful for each day, although, as with anything, the more often and the longer you do it, the better. You can start the day with it, do it over lunch and/or go to bed with it. You can be grateful for the same things every day, or different ones. Remember your confirmation bias and that what you give your attention to grows, so the more you do it, the more you'll see things to be grateful for.

Reasons to be grateful are actually everywhere when you intentionally try to connect with them more. You'll see so many simple wonders of life, so many blessings to count, 'ordinary days', 'ordinary jewels' and 'ordinary angels'. Find beauty in, even treasure, the 'mundane'. You can be grateful for: nature, your senses, friends, family, your body, material possessions, your breath, past experiences and memories, future potential and exciting fantasy, being free from pain, being free, the wind in the trees, the sun on your face or your freedom to choose, walk, run, create, listen, speak and imagine.

Being alive might be reason enough to smile, no? You can parent gratefully; work gratefully; eat, travel, exercise, wake up and go to bed gratefully. Be grateful for the fact that nothing terrible happened today, because, if it had, your life would be in turmoil at the moment. Be a grateful friend, lover, parent or employee. **Live gratefully.** This closes the gaps opened up by threat/reward and will give you a gentle, healthier reward than the usual familiar substances and behaviours.

As we'll see in Principle 4, unhelpful threat/reward can also distort your relationship with your body. It can be really helpful to reconnect, with gratitude, with how extraordinary and awesome your body is. It's a constant and grounding resource for your gratitude practice. Try to make a conscious effort to check in with every part of your body when you can and, if it's the case, be grateful that it's pain free. Because if you were in pain, again, it'd be the only thing you could think about at this moment.

Gratitude for your body also focuses your attention on the present moment, which is a powerful balanced connection tool, as we'll see in Principle 5. Rather than feeling impatience at the person walking slowly in front of you with the walking stick, move to balanced connection by using this moment to say thanks in your head that you don't need one yet. While you wait, appreciate.

As well as gratitude for your own being, body and life, try to think of all the reasons you can be grateful for others. Deliberately draw your attention to the good that's in front of you everywhere. You now know that your brain isn't built to consistently do this unless you make it happen. I deal with relationships with others generally in Principle 8 (page 147).

Forgiveness

When threat is too dominant, you might tend to hold onto grudges and resentments. It'll want you to keep records of past wrongs and will pull them into the present if it can't find anything to worry about today. In balanced connection though, you'll be working to forgive yourself – to remember without anger – because that's really the best way to take care of yourself.

You might feel guilty about the way you've behaved in the past because of threat/reward dominance and it's important to acknowledge that and even allow yourself to feel it a bit. At some point though, you'll want to move on and leave it in the past. Threat has difficulty forgiving and letting go of the anger you feel about what happened, probably because it believes that somehow you let yourself, or another person, get away with it, even win, if you forgive. That, by forgiving, you agree that what happened was okay/right. But, of course, what happened may never be okay/right. To be more in balanced connection though, you'll want to stop it carrying on hurting you in this present moment. If you don't try to do that, it's the threat gift that'll keep on giving forever in your life.

Accept you've always done your best, that there were no reliable crystal balls and/or fortune tellers available. **No regrets, no records of wrongs.** You're never getting the time back, but it's enough to take the lesson of whatever the difficult experience was, forgive yourself, decide how you might do it differently next time and do what you can to achieve that. The reason you did the things you did is because that's what humans will do if we're not shown another way. And you probably weren't shown another way – do you remember exploring many, or any, of the things we're looking at in this book at school, or with your friends and family as you grew up?

And if you're not at a stage where you want to forgive yourself yet, then the next best place is for you to at least **accept it** as part of your **past** now. To enable this, I'd suggest you write down your story of what happened and the effect it had on you – a story characterised by empathy, particularly for you, and also, where possible, for the other person involved. This should help you to put the events into context in terms of your whole life story, hopefully allowing some peace with it now. You can then get on with investing your precious energy in a more balanced connection.

Patience

Patience is another powerful way to connect more with yourself and others. Panic button, 'do it **now**' threat and 'meet my craving **now**' reward might mean you've noticed you lack patience. You'll want to nurture it now. The more patient you are, the more you're able to keep connected to yourself and others. As to how to do this and maintain balanced connection generally, the key is keeping both **calm and alive**, and we'll look specifically at this in Principle 5 (page 127).

Humility

As you know, the superiority of threat doesn't like the thought of you just being 'good enough' or just like other people. It wants specialness, searches for perfection and/or can criticise others for their seeming 'inferiority' or 'superiority'. Humility is therefore a word you may need to hold in mind here, while also bearing in mind that threat can use it as another stick to beat you with.

A balanced connection view is that, while you know the important space you inhabit in the world, no one is less beautiful, or more special, than anyone else. As great, irreplaceable and unique as you are, you're one part of this great, interconnected body of humanity; a part of something much bigger than you and a world that doesn't revolve around you. Which is quite a relief, actually, because it means you can now just get on and do your own thing.

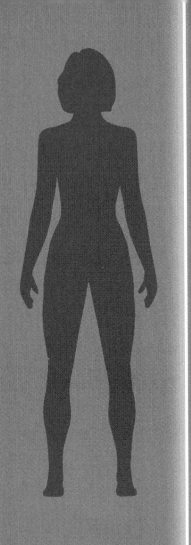

dreams

daydreams

inspiration

opinions

beliefs

values

behaviour

body

feelings

thoughts

4 Know
YOURSELF

CHAPTER 9

Principle 4: Know Yourself

When threat dominates, you may often be trying to understand and work other people out without really fully knowing, understanding and appreciating yourself. This makes life much more difficult than it needs to be. To connect with/love yourself, you first need to know **who you are – who you're in love with**. Threat/reward's hyper-vigilance to your outside world doesn't leave much time to look inwards at the real you. Too much threat can leave a void inside and, when you do turn inwards, it's often just to register an inferior/superior comparison and find a problem. If you don't know who you are, you may be too reliant on, and care too much about, what other people tell you you are. Reward, as you know, always goes outward for reward, suggesting that what already exists inside you just isn't enough.

If you are living with threat as a dominant trait, you might describe feeling 'lost' and 'stuck', not really knowing who you are after decades, all the while being able to rattle off 10 things you don't like about yourself. It paints an unappealing self-portrait and writes a lifeless autobiography. If reward controls you rather than the other way around, you'll overlook all that's good as it is, as you crave for what could be.

Therefore, a key way for you to move more to balanced connection is to turn **inwards**. You need to get to know yourself better, to look at yourself through your new, more caring lens. To try to see yourself in the way that threat/reward caregivers didn't. To have a fuller appreciation of who you are, what you're not and what you have. In balanced connection you need an **expansive** view; **the sea and not just the wave**. Threat knows what you should and ought to do, but, because it disconnects you from your felt experience/body (see Principle 4), it often compromises your ability to know what you'd actually **like** to do. Unless, of course, it's reward's beliefs that you mostly just want to get rich, laid or wrecked.

It's worth bearing in mind where your positive self-image and self-esteem were meant to have come from. As you know, it's largely early caregivers who held up the mirror to you and told you who you were. They said whether, or not, you were worthwhile, valuable and lovable, and which particular aspects of your personality, or qualities, fitted that bill. But, caregivers dominated by threat/reward are often either frightened, frightening or switched off. With poor self-image themselves, they can lack the qualities necessary to build anything at all, except an awareness of limitations – things you should or shouldn't do – and maybe how to temporarily alter their state with reward. This can leave you without the toolkit necessary to build and maintain a helpful and productive self-image.

You've had other people's threat/reward problems imposed on you for too long already, so now it's time to find yourself and work out who you are. What specifically do you need to look at now? What makes you up as a human being? Your thoughts, feelings, behaviours and body are important elements here. So, take each of these bricks that forms part of your whole, look at it with fresh eyes, put it back in place if it works for you and try to work on its replacement over time if it doesn't.

Thoughts and Images

Thoughts and images in your mind are a key definer of your moment-by-moment experience of life. It's estimated that you have between 50,000 and 70,000 thoughts a day and it's believed that 80–95 per cent of them happen under the radar. That's a huge capacity for either the 'heaven' of balanced connection or the 'hell' of dominant threat/reward. You can see thoughts and images as, respectively, the words and pictures you hold in your mind. I'll use the word 'thoughts' throughout this section to cover both words and images. We'll also go on to look at images in more detail in Principle 6 around creative imagination (page 137).

Because threat finds the problem in whatever it looks at, you might say you 'overthink', 'overanalyse', are in your head or 'think too much'. But it's not **that** you think a lot that is the problem in threat/reward, it's **what** you think. You'd have no relationships, career, past, future or sense of self and others without thoughts.

You couldn't read, process experiences, check-in with what's happening with your body, choose, discriminate between what resonates and what doesn't and act on the contents of this book without them. Thoughts organise life, maintain friendships, play fantasy league football, provide nostalgic memories, formulate helpful responses, imagine sexual fantasies, make good decisions, fix cars, write songs and make birthday cakes.

This is, of course, when you're in balanced connection, when thoughts are largely therefore coming from connection and this requires having **control, and therefore choice**, over them. Once you have a balance of helpful threat, reward and connection thoughts, although you'll probably have fewer than when threat dominates, you'll likely not be able to get enough of thoughts. Like all aspects of you in balanced connection, they'll be your ally.

As you've seen, threat/reward naturally hijack thought as they're biologically meant to. Every thought you have sends a chemical into your body that affects your body/feelings. You know that threat thoughts held in mind will then be experienced in life due to your biases. People who believe you're not meant to enjoy your work, for example, are unlikely to ever enjoy what they do and people who believe everyone is fundamentally selfish and self-serving are often in relationships with highly narcissistic people. This is **the virtual reality of too much threat/reward thinking**. Threat thoughts of permanence, pervasiveness, hopelessness and helplessness are, of course, untrue. However, when delivered consistently and as truth, they become self-fulfilling prophecies. Try to be aware that **if you think it all the time, it had better be what you want**.

You know why threat thoughts might be more powerful and convincing than connection ones. That threat thoughts seem intensely real and factual is reflected in the fact you may sometimes feel guilty for having them. You might feel guilty for **even thinking** you dislike someone or for having a sexual fantasy about someone other than your partner. But guilt because of a thought? Because of some miniscule, often randomly generated, blip from a few of your trillion neurons? From 1/60,000th of your thought day? In balanced connection you can try to let go of feeling guilty for a thought, or feelings for that matter. Guilt should only be reserved for things you **do or don't do** that cross your moral compass.

Thoughts, from whichever part of you, are just a little passing piece of your human experience. Like the sound of a car driving past or an itch. They're only a collective idea you've learned to hold on to, reusing the limited data you've taken in to date. In balanced connection, you need to try not to collude with any overinflated sense of the importance of threat/reward thoughts. You know they often just aren't meant to be taken that seriously, in spite of the fervent hype.

You need to relate to thoughts as **an aspect** of your being **rather than being them**. Just because a threat/reward thought intrudes, is obsessive or unwanted, doesn't mean it's any truer than a connection one. Your thoughts are an invitation. Acceptance of them by you is optional. You can't stop a bird landing on your head, but you can stop it making a nest. So you need to choose to hold on to thoughts when they're helpful connection, reward and threat, and, as for the rest, try to let them pass like clouds across a blue sky, or leaves floating downstream on a river.

Of course, this is all often easier said than done. Your unwanted thoughts, like too much threat/reward generally, will probably need to be gently, actively and consistently managed for quite some time before balanced connection drops nicely into your unconscious and becomes your default. How do you observe and then test the helpfulness, or otherwise, of thoughts? You need to develop and strengthen **your guide** – your main supporter of this whole journey to balanced connection – which we'll explore in detail in Principle 5 (page 127).

Something that a developed guide will do is enable you to recognise your thoughts, labelling them as they arrive and allowing the unhelpful ones to pass before they make their nest. For example, saying to yourself whether they're 'memory', 'fantasy', 'planning', 'anger', 'comparison', 'superiority', 'inferiority', 'gratitude', 'argument', 'love', 'sex', 'reward', 'connection', 'untrustworthy', 'protective,' 'threat' or 'judging'. You now know threat thoughts have some particular qualities that will make them easier to recognise – they're binary, permanent, pervasive and personal, black-and-white, 'what ifs', 'should haves', catastrophes, 'how dare they', experiencing yourself as victim and life being a series of all-or-nothing absolutes. Try to label your thoughts as they come along, witness and smile at them, and let the unhelpful ones go on their way. It might be that you notice threat thoughts dominate at night or early in the morning. If this is the case, you could go so far as to say to yourself, for example, that between the hours of 8 p.m. and 10 p.m., or for the first hour of the day, what you think and feel is going to be largely threat-based, distorted and therefore untrustworthy.

A helpful technique to practise can also be to rewind your thoughts: think back through your day in reverse, and remember what you were thinking about at any point in time. On your way back from work, for example, try to remember what you were thinking just before you left the office, then rewind to an hour before that to around the time you got a call from your client, then backwards again to when you were checking your social media mid-morning, then back to what you thought when you were showering this morning. This gets you used to treating your thoughts the way they need to be experienced, as just a part of you that you're able to observe and therefore manage.

As well as compassionately relating to the unhelpful threat/reward thoughts and either allowing them to pass or responding calmly and expansively to them, you'll also need to develop your ability to give yourself balanced connection alternatives and to take hold of and expand the connection ones. You know that your brain – possessing no inbuilt, automatic process to identify and expand your connection experiences – is not naturally programmed to turn your good experiences, like that great appraisal or an unprompted warm hug from someone, into neural pathways you can keep going back to. You therefore need to try to deliberately do that now, every day, whenever you remember. By doing this, you'll increase your ability to recognise and grow the good in yourself and others, and be standing on more concrete internal foundations when you face past, present and future experiences.

How do you expand and prolong your fleeting connection moments of happiness and contentment? Unlike the just 'witness and let go' approach to unhelpful threat/reward thoughts, you need to take hold of these connection moments of joy, peace, gratitude, love, pride, etc. and make them much **bigger** in your mind **and** your body. When you feel good about something, actively bring your attention to it and enhance it. A few ways you can notice you're feeling connected are experiencing tears of joy, genuine smiles and laughter, and having goose bumps, 'chills' or the shivers (except when you're frightened, of course).

You need to **lean into** these experiences, make them louder inside you, both in terms of staying longer with the thought **and** by noticing what this good, connected experience **feels** like in and throughout your body. Where do you feel it in your body? What are the sensations like? It's this – really **feeling** good and connected and expanding and intensifying the aliveness you experience as a result – that **installs** it for the future. It's believed that aiming for at least 20 seconds when you do this is all that's needed to make a new connection neural pathway.

This includes times when people flatter and compliment you. Threat typically responds to this with cringing and embarrassment, but it's helpful if you actually cultivate these moments, are receptive to them and repeatedly remind yourself of them afterwards. You can distinguish this from arrogance/superiority because it's not about being better than others, just connecting to and grounding your standalone worth and value, as well as the kindness of others.

When looking at past and traumatic experiences, always remember that, although they took some of your breath, you survived, coped and may have even thrived at times since. You've come this far without much connection to/love of self and what has meant you could do this? What is it about you that you imagine the people **already** in your life like/love about you? If threat believes you're so weak or crazy, such a loser, then how do you manage to do all that you do and be all that you are? Well, most likely, it's with a combination of resilience, sensitivity, strength, resourcefulness, determination, intelligence and more.

If your issue is addiction, try to think about those qualities that 'successfully' acting out your addiction has required over the years: probably resourcefulness, resilience, determination, as well as focus and planning, to name just a few. High anxiety will often come with a quick brain, a keen ear and eye, people-pleasing, sensitivity and conscientiousness that can be really helpful life skills. If you think about narcissism, it may mean you believe you can pretty much do anything, in whatever way you want and that a 'normal life' doesn't **have to** apply to you. If you've approached situations assuming you're better than your 'competition', it could have worked out very well for you at times.

It's likely that in these wounded places you'll find some real gold in terms of your gifts as a human being. Try to find aspects of who you are **now**, the skills/qualities/competencies you **already** possess, to be proud of. Imagine what life could be like if you focus on consistently applying these to behaviours that are in your best interests from this point on. Dominant threat will tell you that this is arrogant, egotistical or self-aggrandising, but try to go ahead and do it anyway.

Try to think in terms of connected creativity when you're thinking about yourself here. This will all sound like words and sentences in your head: everything from simple affirmations about your worth and value, to gratitude for self, to calm, complex, expansive explanations about **all** of your skills and qualities. Affirmations are particularly good, because you're often going to need quick and simple statements to shift from being dominated by threat to living in balanced connection. They're positive statements expressed in the present tense that you can embody. For example:

- 'I am whole, healthy and healing.'
- 'I'm valuable and lovable.'
- 'I am safe and loved.'
- 'I can choose who to trust.'

Over time, and with your deliberate effort, these ways of talking to yourself will become habitual.

You also need to look more deeply beneath your thoughts to see what they're standing on to both find, and, where necessary, replace, any below-the-radar unhelpful threat/reward roots.

These deeper foundations include:

Beliefs

Many thoughts about yourself and the world come from what you believe about these concepts. Whether you call them beliefs, injunctions, old 'agreements', complexes or taboos, the point, as ever, is that you need to make sure they're balanced connection beliefs and not too much from threat/reward.

You're in the shape of the past, of everything you've seen, heard and felt. As I've mentioned, without you being aware of it, your partner today can feel like your childhood caregiver; your boss like your old teachers; and in groups today you might act out your patterns and role from your childhood family. Beliefs you have internalised about yourself and the world are the basis on which you run, or run down, your life. They decide the position you take in any given situation and are therefore hugely important. And some of these might serve you well today. If too much threat/reward has been a part of your story though, a proportion won't.

Let's predict the relationship history and life prospects of someone who believes 'all girls like bad boys', 'life is hard', 'trust no one', 'familiarity breeds contempt', 'we're not meant to enjoy work', 'the world's going to hell in a handcart', 'all couples fight', 'bullying is part of growing up' or 'all men are bastards'. These are relics of a threat/reward past, borne out of a threat/reward caregiver's emotional distress/a heterosexist culture/school bullying/the place you were made to occupy in your family system/a generally threat/reward culture. Due to your biases, they become self-fulfilling prophecies.

If threat/reward are too dominant, without a doubt, you'll have formed and, with your biases, built on, some unsafe toxic beliefs that no longer serve you. Imagine if you're not actually just stupid, lazy, superior, clumsy, boring, weird, the class clown, thick, better than, fiery, weak, ditsy, the funny one, special, the fat one, the rebel, a geek, bad with girls, a loser, crap at relationships, a failure… Imagine living without these self-defeating, unhelpful ceilings and walls. And imagine just how freeing this would be.

Think of how limiting a 'man's man', 'a girlie girl', 'introverted/ extroverted' or a 'bitch' might be in terms of your experience of yourself and others. Begin to take stock of all of your internal beliefs. Who do you think you are? What's that based on? If you don't like a belief, what are you going to believe instead now? How do you define beauty, or strength, or success? What are the concepts of masculine and feminine you're standing on? What does it take to be a 'woman' or a 'man'? Are some of these ideas being used by excessive threat as sticks to beat you with? Do you want to define/limit yourself in these ways anymore when you have such a huge capacity and potential for connected imagination and creativity?

If you have children, do you want your children to have the self-image and/or relationships you have? To feel the same way about their job as you do about yours? If not, then you need to try to change your experience of these things from this point, because however much you, and they, might want things to be different for them, they're going to struggle to make the change if you are not modelling that change for them. They'll most likely only be able to do as you do, not as you say. The best chance of your child being the person you want them to be is to be that person yourself. You need to try to live the life – psychologically and emotionally – that you want them to live and, to do that, you need to make sure your underlying beliefs about yourself and your world are in line with such a life. You want them to love their body/job/partner? **Then do what you can to make sure you love yours.**

Try to explore the beliefs you live by now, so you can stop tiring yourself out with any old threat/reward stories. Identify what your dominant threat/reward beliefs are and choose what you'd prefer to believe about yourself and the world instead. Believe good things are going to happen for you from this point on. Let's be curious and open to all possibilities about who you, others and the world might be. A list of some suggested core beliefs is set out below for you. It might be helpful to spend some time thinking about each of these and notice what they bring up:

Belief	Your Comments
I'm a good person	
I'm a smart person	
I'm a trustworthy person	
I'm an honest person	
I'm okay just the way I am	
I'm safe	
I'm worthy	
I'm lovable	
I belong	
I can take care of myself	
I can trust my judgement	
I can succeed	
I can get what I want	
I deserve to be happy	
I can communicate my emotional needs	
I can choose who to trust	

I can safely show my feelings	
I can empathise with others' needs	
I can trust others to meet my needs	

Some possible narcissistic superiority aside, you are undoubtedly capable of a huge amount more than dominant threat/reward believes you are. You can choose now to respectfully leave your unhelpful threat/reward beliefs with the people they came from and energise yourself with balanced connection beliefs instead. Try to build a narrative of self, and others, that too much threat/reward hasn't previously allowed you. Spend some time taking stock of how far you've come, based largely on the timeline of your achievements, talents and competencies rather than your threat biases. This will help you to build a more balanced, coherent story of your past, present and future.

It can be helpful here to draw a timeline of your life. Draw a horizontal line across an A3 page, write your birth year on the left end of the line and the current year on the right. Then fill in all the important dates, adding colours or symbols to categorise them if you want. These dates could include: births, deaths, romantic relationships, job changes, moves, friendships and, most importantly, all happy times and any successes, awards or achievements. As you create this timeline, reflect and expand on those memories that give you a pleasant feeling and make you smile, as well as the effect on you of those that might have been painful. Reflect on how they all helped you to become the person you are today.

It's possible, with narcissism's special worthlessness, that you've believed some great things about yourself that haven't always been borne out by the reality of your behaviour. Although this might be difficult to accept, realising it will help to set you free from the tendency to believe in a superiority over others that's disconnecting and not therefore self-care. It's all good, because you now know why you've been doing it and that, by working through these principles, you can ensure the reality of your behaviour is actually much closer to any narcissistic fantasy you have about how great you are. You may even find that these fantasies reflect the greatness you'll now be able to consistently achieve in reality, if that's what you want. It'll all come out in the wash as you move more to balanced connection.

Values

Values are what are important to you – the reasons you get up in the morning. They're different to goals, which are targets to be achieved. Values are not 'achieved' – you're always working towards and living them. Values will lie beneath your choices, decisions and behaviours. Again, it's therefore important to recognise whether or not they're consistent with balanced connection.

Your external environment while you were growing up will have told you what must be important, or valuable, to you. Caregivers controlled by threat/reward model threat/reward values. And, incidentally, to rebel today and do the opposite because you didn't like the experience may be just as inauthentic for you. If you walk the line because you're frightened of not being like your caregivers, or refuse to walk the line because you're frightened of being your caregivers, you're still orbiting around them in fear/anger.

When threat/reward dominate, you might often say you 'have everything', but you're still not happy. Some of this will be due to threat's biases and/or reward's struggle to appreciate the beauty in the 'ordinary'. But I think the rest is likely to be due to the meaning threat/reward give to 'having everything' or being 'successful'.

As you know, due to its outward-in and survival preoccupations, threat values only how you appear to others, what they think/feel about you and how you compare to each other. These might actually be the main contexts in which you exist psychologically. This may have resulted in you overly preoccupying about social status, job titles, your physical appearance, being rich and famous, 'who you know', reputation, being recognised, reaching 'the top', respect, notoriety and getting more stuff generally. I believe the distress people experience as a result of excessive social media use and the 'addiction' they may have to it is all because of this.

Parents in balanced connection want their children to be content and fulfilled; parents controlled by threat/reward might primarily want them to get a 'good' job that makes a lot of money. The latter are what threat/reward believe show your environment how worthwhile and valuable you are. You might stand, or fall, on the size of a bank balance, your nose, a party invite or an Instagram like. And, yes, people might be better disposed to you if have a good hair day, but you're often going to struggle to be happy and fulfilled if you believe your worth and value **begins and ends** with your external appearance. And what happens as age gradually takes youth, fitness and your competitive edge off you? Or if illness does it suddenly? For its part, unhelpful reward will overly value 'fun', short-term reward and not feeling 'bored'.

Therapy rooms are full of wealthy material girls and boys, who have worked hard for decades at stuff that isn't actually important to them. Taught mainly just to fight and to win, money has bought them 'everything', but little of real value to them. In fact, it may have done them some harm in terms of their happiness and well-being. They've lost sight of connection, of what's really important once the basic needs are met, as the money piles up, struggling to enjoy and get any kind of meaning from the things they have. Always wondering why the dream of happiness that was promised by caregivers, advertisers or employers as the result of having lots of material possessions or status just doesn't seem to be consistently true.

You need to look at your current values now. Look at the list overleaf and tick all those values that are important to you. Then choose five that are your priorities. As you know, too much threat often makes prioritising difficult, so try to spend some time doing this.

Accepting myself		Being resilient	
Accepting others		Being competent	
Being creative		Communicating my physical and emotional needs	
Being warm to others		Communicating my feelings	
Being a good partner		Developing friendships	
Being a good parent		Developing practical skills	
Being a good friend		Developing knowledge	
Being kind		Enjoying life	
Being ambitious		Enjoying rest, silence and solitude	
Being physically fit		Expressing gratitude to others	
Being responsible		Feeling content and happy	
Being trustworthy and honest		Feeling safe	
Being loved by others		Feeling accomplished	
Being respectful of my-self and others		Feeling calm and at peace	
Being loyal		Having fun	
Being mindful		Having integrity	
Being spontaneous		Having meaning and purpose	
Being true to who I am		Having equanimity	

Being patient		Helping other people	
Being in control		Having empathy for others	
Being consistent in all areas of my life		Having clarity	
Being adventurous		Having structure	
Being financially secure		Inspiring other people	
Being brave		Knowing my physical and emotional needs	
Being principled		Knowing what I'm feeling	
Being good humoured		Loving others	
Being spiritual		Learning and exploring new things	
Being optimistic		Spending time in nature	

Once you've decided on five from the above list, try to hold them in mind in all that you do in your day. What do you want to be important to you today, to make sure you have a real sense of meaning, purpose and passion in your life? Maybe even choose a photo or image that represents your "top" value now and make it your phone screensaver, so you're always reminded of it. What if you had just six months to live – what would you do? How do you define success, happiness and what's 'productive'? If threat tells you that enjoying rest and solitude is 'lazy', maybe you can now believe instead that it's a valuable, productive use of your time. What's consistent with, and important to, the more connected person you want to be? Interestingly in this regard, you may not need to aim sky-high in terms of this more connected person – studies by Susan Fiske and Amy Cuddy have found that we judge others mainly by just two benchmarks: their warmth and their competence. Warmth seems to me to be present when we're connected to others and competence when we're connected to self.

Opinions

Another possible sign of unhelpful threat is a compromised relationship with opinions: you may not know what yours are and/or lack courage to express them or make them too important. With threat's primary survival preoccupation, it makes sense to keep your head below the parapet. You might always bite your tongue, afraid to say something wrong, even tolerate and smile at views that are potentially repugnant to you. Your opinions can go unformed and unsaid for so long you even give up connection to them.

Again, growing up, caregivers dominated by threat may have given the message that a different opinion is a problem, identifying it, in the same way threat sees everything, as a potential threat to their fragile sense of self. You need to be curious as to whether you've taken on a threat belief that you must always be submissive in order to survive in this world.

Due to the perceived self-worthlessness, problem-focus, anger, struggle to self-soothe and tolerate difference that characterise threat, the other possibility is that you take a difference of opinion too personally and/or amplify its importance more than is helpful. People can go from hero to zero for you because they dare to disagree.

You can see in both of the above situations how threat can cause problems. But, like beliefs and values, opinions are part of who you are. They're internal boundaries (see Principle 9), ways to assess integrity and guidance points on your moral compass that can be distorted when threat/reward are too dominant. They make you potentially different and therefore interesting to others. So, you need to notice what they are and maybe over time try to calmly express them without threat taking differences of opinion personally.

As with any behavioural move to turn threat down, it will be difficult at the start to voice a potentially controversial opinion as your amygdala fires off. But that will come with time, patience and trust as the confrontations and annihilations threat fears don't actually happen. It's important to hold this in mind when others have different opinions to you. A different opinion is not something for threat to overcome. You can yield, or agree to differ; you don't have to win. And if you're around people who, as an ongoing pattern of behaviour, attack you for having a different opinion, they may be better being moved out of your life (see Principle 8). Similarly, if there are those in your life that hold and express opinions repugnant to you, it may be taking balanced connection care of yourself to move them out of your life.

You need to know now what you stand for, to avoid falling for everything if that's what been happening. Some opinions will be there, hidden beneath your threat/reward concerns. Others you may need to work out. Read some news and listen to talk radio to see what resonates with and triggers for you. Over time, as with everything in these principles, as you do this, you're gradually colouring in the image of your true self.

Inspirations

If you are controlled by threat/reward, either you may not have an answer to the question of who inspires you, or you might venerate people who are rich and famous or aggressive, or both. In my view, needing to admire the rich, the powerful, the physically strong, the beautiful, the aggressive and the famous or notorious, **solely** because they are those things may belong to an age which has now passed. You don't need to dominate others, or be able to win in a gang-fight to the death anymore to live a safe, happy and successful life today. This isn't Game of Thrones.

Self-preservation is not the place of balanced, connected, inspirational heroes and heroines. Neither are its superiority/ inferiority complexes that mean people can 'make' you feel bad. When reward controls you, you might often see others as a means to an end, rather than as an end in themselves.

Maybe try to think about who inspires you, who's a balanced, connected hero for you. And if there's no one at the moment, just keep an eye out. Being curious and interested in other people's stories – really looking for balanced people to admire – is another way to connect with your internal world and your own wonderful humanity. You may even realise you're recognising in others your own admirable qualities that you struggle to appreciate when threat/reward dominate. And, as you move to balanced connection, I think it's likely that one day people will say you inspire them, if you don't already that is.

Dreams and daydreams

Your daydreams can tell you more about yourself and what you want and need. When threat controls you, they might feature catastrophes and rehearsing arguments. When you are controlled by reward, they'll be dominated by euphoric recall and/or fantasies. Your daydreams might also be the way you try to compensate for threat's insecurity, fantasising about being powerful, beating others and/or being admired by them. As with all aspects of yourself in this journey, it's important you try to approach them with gentle **curiosity**, despite threat's disapproval or embarrassment.

The dreams you have when sleeping can also let you know what's happening below the radar, when your conscious defences of the day are down. A lot has been written about the meaning of dreams. Some people believe certain symbols in dreams represent age-old themes of human experience; others see dreams as your brain trying to resolve unfinished emotional business of the day; and others suggest every person or thing present in your dream is actually an aspect of you. Generally, though, I believe noticing and being interested in dreams is another way to pay attention/connect to your internal landscape and to better understand, relate to and appreciate yourself and others.

Look inside and be curious about your thoughts, values, beliefs, opinions, inspirations, daydreams and dreams. Try to get to know your internal habits and patterns and where your mind wanders, to become more self-aware and connected to yourself. This helps with distancing yourself from dominant threat/reward's never-ending outward focus and disconnection. Instead of spending your time-limited, precious life shaped by other people's threat/reward from the past, you can now choose your own balanced connection experience.

Feelings

As you can see from the above, too much threat/reward distort your relationship with your vital feeling function and, because feelings are bodily experiences, your body. Threat's survival instinct and reward's preoccupation with 'highs' mean you might have lost contact with your body's nuanced feelings a long time ago. As threat dominated, everything else had to defer to its distortions and biases. Threat might, in fact, use the words 'emotional' or 'sensitive' in a disparaging way, as it turns against another key part of your experience, often pushing it outside of your conscious control in the process.

In balanced connection, 'emotional' isn't a criticism. Whether they're your emotions, or another's, try to hold in mind that connecting with your emotions, giving them a level playing field with your thoughts and body, is key to living a more lived life.

On a basic level, your feelings either tell you what to physically go towards or what to come away from – whether you're in or you're out. Threat often separates your feelings from your thoughts, in the hope that you can think more clearly to survive without the interruption of feelings. With a lost connection with your range of feelings, you've lost the important messages that feelings, and therefore your body, can give you about what's happening in your life. This actually weakens the value of your thoughts, leaving you more psychologically unsafe, and in turn reinforcing unhelpful threat/reward.

For example, you can see this working if you have a job which isn't actually something you enjoy doing most of the time. You carry on solely because it's 'a good job' and you believe others will think you're 'a failure' if you stop – these are threat/status reward thoughts in action. Continuing in this job means you often have to override the messages you're getting from your feelings. You may have been used to doing this for years to survive in your family home, or at school, which is why it's second nature. The trouble is, if, as a pattern of behaviour, you don't see your feelings as a key indicator of what you should and shouldn't be doing, they'll no longer indicate to you. You're left just doing stuff, or not doing stuff, based on dominant threat/reward. If you don't know what you feel, you'll struggle to organise your behaviour and prioritise experience in a way that makes you happy, just 'going through the motions' instead, unsure what's real for you and what isn't.

How do you choose to do things you enjoy when you've lost contact with feelings of enjoyment? When you therefore don't know what makes you excited, or feel passionate or proud anymore? How do you know whether to do this, or that, or see more, or less, of a person, take this, or that, job, without access to your range of feelings? You may just be left basing those decisions on threat's frightened/frightening or reward's fun/boring perspectives. How are you going to turn threat and anger down to have a more connected life, if you're not always aware that you're feeling them?

One of the first things I do if someone comes to me to talk about anger management is to ask them to notice how many times a day they're annoyed or angry. Without exception, they usually haven't realised they're actually chronically annoyed most of the time, anything between 10–15 times a day. Why don't you do the same out of interest? Try to think of how many times you felt annoyed, impatient, frustrated, agitated, irritated or angry yesterday. It'll probably surprise you, as anger makes the external 'perpetrator' your focus rather than your own internal landscape.

Importantly, in order to move unhelpful reward out of your life, you have to be able to notice that addictive behaviour doesn't actually **feel** good most of the time. Your feelings throughout the whole addictive cycle – the numbness, the disappointment, the guilt, the shame – are miles away from entertainment and true reward. You're going to need to know the felt/bodily difference between eating/having sex because you're hungry/horny and engaging in those behaviours because you feel anxious/angry or numb. You'll also need to try to start noticing the more everyday experiences that can give you lower level, but more sustainable, joy and pleasure if you're going to move unhelpful reward out of your life.

You'll be familiar with the cliché of therapists asking their clients 'How are you feeling?', but we do this because feelings are usually the parts of ourselves that most of us know least as we come through childhood. As we discussed in Chapter 3, depression is not about being sad all the time; it's about lacking vitality, being under-aroused, with a lack of connection to feelings/body. If you look at all the threat/reward conditions that bring people into therapy, they're often about feelings/the body fighting back and making a person change course in an unplanned and distressing way. For example, someone no longer being able to function at work because of anxiety, or someone who hasn't been aware of their anger assaulting another person in a road rage incident, directed into therapy to avoid a life-changing criminal record.

As we've seen, your lack of connection with feeling may have been set up in childhood, possibly with caregivers driven by threat/reward. You might have heard the injunctions of 'boys don't cry', 'man-up', 'suck it up', 'get a grip', 'don't be silly, you're fine', 'pull yourself together', 'get over it' and 'put a smile on your face'. These may all have led to hiding your feelings and the clear message that some feelings are acceptable and therefore 'lovable' and others aren't – 'laugh and the world laughs with you, cry and you cry alone'. Often anger is less acceptable for girls and sadness for boys. Threat, with its binary outlook and preoccupation with survival, labels some feelings as 'weak' and showing 'no feeling' as 'strong'. It might label love as 'sentimental', 'slushy' and 'soft' and say that tears of sadness are just 'self-pity', 'turning on the waterworks', 'self-indulgent', 'fake', 'babyish', 'manipulative' and 'crocodile tears'.

Disconnection from feelings/the body might also have been encouraged where a caregiver dominated by threat worried how your anger, or even excitement, would appear to the outside world. Often it's because your caregiver couldn't relate to, contain, feel and/or process their own feelings. As you know, if your feelings tipped your caregiver into anger, or anxiety, you'll have soon learned to repress and deny those feelings. Over time it wasn't even worth feeling your feelings in your body that probably wanted you to get out of there at times. And if you disconnect from feeling pain, you might also disconnect from the connection feelings of love, peace and joy that you want.

The split from feelings/the body also often gets strengthened at work. Your career can meet important emotional needs: providing status you value; feeling part of a wider community; enabling you to achieve things you're proud of; and giving you a sense of purpose. But, dominant threat can also be a well-paid asset, even requirement, in some careers. A constant drive for reward similarly so. If you refused to give up 'spare time' that could be spent connecting with yourself and loved ones, you might be much less appealing to your clients/customers/company's share-holders. Threat/reward qualities of impulsive risk-taking, lack of empathy, narcissism, even sociopathy, are often tolerated – and rewarded – for their profit-making potential. It's believed that the job title with the most sociopaths is CEO.

Connecting more to the full range of your feelings is going to be an essential part of your move to balanced connection. You're going to need to try to make your feelings an ally, to bring them, and therefore your body, fully back into your awareness and back under control. As with everything, the more you give your attention to them, the more they grow and the stronger they get.

In order to connect more with your feelings, maybe ask yourself, wherever and whenever possible, **what** you're feeling. You could make a mental note to do this at least three times a day, even set a reminder on your phone to prompt you. Notice the thoughts that go with the feeling and any physiological effect you notice it has on your body. Does that slight stomach ache mean you're hungry? Or have you been tightening your abdomen because you're under sustained stress? If you notice it, you can then manage it in the moment with some calming breathing and avoid reacting angrily towards a colleague in a way you might regret.

Perhaps even more importantly than noticing when you're in threat, you also need to know how you feel when you're connected to others and vice versa. What does connection love/care/affection actually **feel like in your body**? What are the sensations?

When asked what you're feeling, you might often respond with a **thought**, just prefaced with the words 'I felt that…' or 'I felt like…'. For example, 'I felt that it wasn't the place for me' or 'I felt like she didn't like me.' In balanced connection, you'll have fuller language around your feelings. This language is a way to connect with them in relationships with both yourself and others. Your feeling will be one word: 'angry', 'sad', 'ashamed', 'calm', 'frustrated', 'excited', although the feelings may come one after another in quick succession. Rather than saying you felt 'upset', 'emotional' or 'stressed', maybe be more specific. By 'upset' do you mean sad, fearful or annoyed? By 'stressed' do you mean frustrated, fearful or annoyed? And emotional? There are hundreds of words you can use to describe your emotions.

Once you know what the feeling is, you can then manage it and therefore your body. In the case of threat feelings, it's important to do this or you'll have a tendency to react in an unhelpful way. But this isn't about criticising yourself for these threat feelings. For balanced connection, you need a compassionate and empathetic relationship with your feelings, not the repression, disconnection and denial of threat/reward. Once you've recognised the feeling you're experiencing in your body, acknowledge that whatever it is is okay. Try to ask yourself why you're feeling it and whether or not you should respond to it. Is threat possibly distorting your perception with its biases?

If you realise you're angry with someone because threat has told you a horror story that's probably not actually true, you need to be able to gently give the feelings a nod, smile and allow them to pass on their way without feeding them (see Principle 5). I don't think voicing **every** frightened and angry thought is a good idea, it's important to run it past your internal guide first, which we'll look at more in Principle 5. If it's a connection feeling of passion, love, joy or excitement you're having, as we saw in the section on 'Thoughts' above, try to practise really taking hold of these and savouring them throughout your body.

Just a note about tears. As you move further into balanced connection, you're likely to feel a lot of sadness. Crying can be associated with depression, but actually I believe tears are often a really good thing. Tears can signify connection to self and others. Try to see them as a psychological success, a sign of strength, because they usually mean you're connecting with love, a sense of loss of love, or grief for what might have been, either now or in your childhood. When you cry during a film or a piece of music, it's probably love, or sorrow (loss of love), you're experiencing. So, rather than stopping yourself, try not to swallow the feeling down, tell yourself 'this is what love feels like', breathe into it, relax your throat and chest and make it bigger. Tears aren't from an endless reservoir that keeps filling up and you may already have noticed you often feel better after you cry.

It's important not to apologise for tears anymore. See it as your right, even your duty, to cry. Tears also generally prompt love and care from others, unlike threat feelings of anger and hatred. So just smile and wave at threat messages that tell you that it's self-indulgent or weak to cry, or that something upsetting is in the past and you shouldn't care anymore. If a feeling hasn't been expressed, it'll be held until it is, so maybe allow yourself to cry for overdue pain, even decades after the events. There's no time limit for this kind of connected self-care. Cry for the fact that you've lived some of your life in lots of unnecessary distress, due to circumstances outside of your control. Cry for what that's meant for the people around you more recently. You all deserved better, including your threat/reward caregivers. That's got to be sad right?

As with thoughts, in balanced connection you need to be aware of your feelings, so you can have choice. You don't want to be consumed by them, acting them out outside of your consciousness, or struggling to live a life that ignores them. Try to think of them as waves, carefully choosing which ones to surf. Like thoughts, over time you'll be better able to manage your feelings and know that you can largely feel whatever you want to feel, whenever you want to feel it.

Ongoing practices like daily journaling, paying attention to dreams and daydreams, mindfulness and therapy can all help improve connection with your feelings/body, as well as thoughts. I'll look at mindfulness and therapy in Principle 5. You might also want to take an 'emotional inventory' of your life to get some idea of whether your emotional needs and wants are being met at the moment. If I asked you what your financial and physical needs are, you'd probably give me quite a quick answer. However, if I asked what your emotional needs and wants are, this could take much longer if threat/reward are controlling you. Below are some possible emotional needs, which I'd like you to score from 1 to 10 (with 10 meaning the need is completely met and 0 meaning it's not met at all). If you give any of these a score of less than 5, they're likely to be priority areas for your attention now.

Emotional needs	Score from 0–10
Relationship with self	
Do you feel safe and secure in your life?	
Do you feel in control of your thought/feelings/behaviours?	
Do you feel in control of your life?	
Do you feel like you have meaning and purpose in life?	
Do you value what you do with your time?	
Do you enjoy what you do with your time?	
Do you believe you're good at the things you spend time doing?	
Are you sometimes trying new things and stretching yourself?	
Do you get enough opportunity to relax and reflect alone?	
Are you achieving things that you're proud of?	
Do you have a future that you're looking forward to?	
Relationships with others	
Do you feel loved by some good people?	
Do you know people you can trust?	
Can you be who you really are with some people in your life?	
Do you give other people enough attention?	

Continues overleaf

Do you get enough attention from other people?	
Are you able to forgive other people and let go of grudges and resentments?	
Are you in an intimate relationship (one in which you feel truly understood, accepted and loved by another person)?	
Do you feel like you belong somewhere?	
Are you contributing to the wider community/world?	

Once you've identified these priority areas, maybe take each one and think about the steps you might take to move your score up a couple of notches. If you gave a '4' to feeling in control of your life, perhaps ask yourself what would need to happen to move that up to a '6'. Having more control over your finances in your relationship? Researching job opportunities and/or updating your CV? Changing your exercise plan? You could review them each weekend; see what's changed in the past week and what might be different next week and how. Importantly, also try to think about why you've given it a '4', i.e., think about what makes up 1–4 of this score. As you know, grounding the good that's here already is really connecting.

Behaviour

With threat's tendency to preoccupy righteously about other people's unhelpful behaviours and possibly justify your own, in balanced connection you need to be aware that how **you DO** life is of key importance and that other people remember you for the things that you **say and do.**

You've seen how much threat/reward can distort your perception of self – either diminishing you or leading you to believe in a greatness/specialness that may not always be borne out by your behaviour. You may believe you're a great friend, partner and/or parent, but, taking your balanced connection definition of love, is this actually how you consistently behave?

Threat/reward are not the places of curiosity about your behaviours; they're autopilot behaviour. When threat is too dominant, you may often do things because you 'have to' or 'should', based on generations-old beliefs. When you are controlled by reward, you repeat the same behavioural cycles to escape psychological pain and/or to simulate aliveness. You therefore need to take a full and honest look at what you actually **do** today, as ever, focusing on whether your current behaviours support threat/reward or balanced connection.

In terms of connection with both self and others and inwards-out behaviours, what do you do that's specifically about taking care of yourself? What do you do to relax and reward yourself? What are your hobbies, if any? What are your competencies/what are you good at doing? What are the goals you're working towards? Can you put together a bucket list of things you still want to do, places you still want to see, things you still want to learn and people you still want to meet? Is it self-care to carry on with the work you're doing? How do you manage your finances? Are you leaving decisions over important things, such as finances or what you do in your spare time, to someone else (therefore being more outward-in than may be helpful)? How are you specifically going to improve connection with your body? How do you exercise? You may spend a lot of time doing, but when are you just being? What's your sleep like? Do you drink enough water? Are you taking care of your nutrition? Do you practise mindfulness/meditation? How much time do you spend in nature? What kind of media are you consuming?

In terms of connection with others, do the things you do in your spare time bring you into contact with like-minded people? Who do you regularly come into contact with? In relation to contact with others via cyberspace, it's worth bearing in mind here the possible hidden 'filter bubble' that may be governing your contact with the world. This was a phrase coined to describe the narrowing down of who and what you see on the Internet by website algorithms predicting what you'd like to see based on the sites you visit. Over time, you only get shown those viewpoints that agree with yours. Couple this with your brain's natural negativity and confirmation biases and it may mean you're sitting in a virtual echo chamber dominated, outward-in, by threat/reward, rather than being shown a balanced, expansive view of the world. Of course, this can very much work in your favour if your time spent on the net is being used to build and sustain a life based on connection with self and others, but it's worth being mindful of this either way.

Have you chosen a job or do things outside of work that contribute to the wider community in some way and/or involve being part of a group? Because of threat's tendency to isolate and avoid, it's important to notice which behaviours might bring you into contact with (balanced connection) others and cultivate them. Whether it's an exercise class, book club, singing along at a concert with 50,000 others or a therapy group, the experience of being part of a group of people doing the same thing, and the synchronicity/attunement with others this hopefully leads to, is powerful connection behaviour for you.

Something you might find helpful to bear in mind here is that communication in your body's nervous system is via chemicals, and connection behaviours generally produce feel-good chemicals, such as serotonin, endorphins and dopamine. When threat dominates it's largely the stress hormones – cortisol and adrenalin – that come to the fore. As ever, it's all about balance – some stress hormone is fine and necessary to get things done, but if you're looking for a greater sense of well-being and happiness, really focus on those behaviours that are about the feel-good chemicals, like spending time around people you love, completing goals/quests, walks in nature and being creative. As always, you need to bear in mind here reward's tendency to hijack feel-good behaviours, which we'll explore further in Principle 7 (page 129).

Body

Another key way to balanced connection is through your body. As we've seen above, excessive threat always forces 'problems' to the top of your internal hierarchy, often leading to you losing some of your connection with your feelings/body.

From a physiological point of view, when threat/reward are at the fore, your nervous system is out of balance. Your nervous system is made up of your sympathetic nervous system and your parasympathetic nervous system. Your sympathetic nervous system is responsible for your danger 'fight or flight' response, tensing your body up and preparing for its threat behaviours. Your parasympathetic nervous system let's you 'rest and digest', or 'feed and breed', when the danger is gone.

If your nervous system is over-aroused and your sympathetic nervous system is too active, this might result in impulsivity, reckless behaviour, reactivity, agitation and feeling uncomfortable in your own skin. If your parasympathetic nervous system is engaged so much that you're under-aroused, you're likely to experience low energy, depression and a feeling of hopelessness and helplessness. In balanced connection, you'll need to think in terms of making sure that this sympathetic/parasympathetic nervous system see-saw is not weighted too much at either end and, instead, you're maintaining an equilibrium, or **balance**, that can be summed up in you most often feeling **both calm and alive**.

You can see how much the body suffers when threat/reward dominate. Threat is a profoundly physical/physiological experience, with your body usually running on stress hormones that put pressure on your heart and disrupt precious sleep. You'll typically be either wired or tired. You can see that behavioural and substance addictions, compulsive over-exercising leading you to exercise on injuries, overworking setting up health **versus** wealth, eating disorders, obesity, stress, bigorexia, obsessive compulsive disorders, self-harm, suicide, body dysmorphia, trichotillomania (compulsive hair pulling), health anxiety, chronic anger, anxiety generally and depression, all physically damage the body and the person's relationship with it.

Threat might also subtly manifest in you holding your body in the ways it believes will keep you safe – in a state of fighting back at unseen enemies. These can include hunching over/forward, rotating your shoulders rather than sitting/standing up straight; quick, shallow breathing high up in your chest; walking with your head tipped forward and down; frowning; clenching your jaw; and balling your fists.

Your body might also have become one of threat's imagined enemies. It'll view your body like it would any other part of your experience; what are its flaws and imperfections and how do these 'threaten' your ongoing survival? How might your body expose you to ridicule, or disapproval, from others, or 'make' you inferior to them? Or how can it make you superior to others? In the process, threat/reward will mean you'll get used to taking your body completely for granted. For threat, if it doesn't hurt, or result in an external change that others can see, you don't have to worry about it and for reward, if it doesn't give you a high, what's the point anyway?

Without being aware of it, you might be treating your body as something to be used, controlled, enhanced, hidden, exposed, knocked into shape, reduced and/or increased in size, just to reduce fear/increase pleasure and status. Your bodily functions, feelings and the process of ageing might have become sources of shame, embarrassment and fear, separating you from, and setting you against, your physical form and its natural, unavoidable, processes. You might feel uncomfortable in your own skin, even at times disgusted by your body. You might also ride your body into the ground for pleasure and reward; too much alcohol, too much rich food, working too hard. Life may have become a largely 'out of body experience'.

Threat can also use your body to support a superiority complex and reward to give you a 'win'. Your body might be brought in to inflate, or reduce, in comparison to other people: shown off in tight clothes to support 'better than', projecting onto people that they must be happy because they're thin, or unhappy because they're not thin and expecting everyone to be doing the same to you.

How do you experience your body in balanced connection? Well, try to hold in mind that your body is much more than just a reward and/or survival system. You need to see how breathtaking, beautiful and complex it is. Think of all the processes going on without complaint, or need for control and approval as you read this: hair and nails growing, oxygen transporting, waste producing, warmth creation, blood flow, skin regenerating, liver and kidneys processing, coordinating, breathing, seeing, hearing, tasting, smelling, touching, feeling and thinking.

In balanced connection you'll need to draw your attention as often as you can to how awesome your body is and all that it does for you. You need to try to value it, to listen to it, even love it. You'll be going to the gym to celebrate everything your body is capable of, rather than as a punishment for something you've eaten. As you look for ways to uncoil and unwind from the clutches of threat/reward, taking care of your body is the easiest way to calm and soothe yourself and connect with your aliveness. By doing so, you'll find it easier to stay in connection with all aspects of yourself and with others.

When you receive, or give, physical affection, the touch produces the feel-good chemical oxytocin, known as the 'love' or 'cuddle' hormone. This reduces your stress hormones (you can't be producing both at the same time) and makes everything feel better. Holding hands, hugging, massage and warm showers all change your state to connection by triggering the production of your feel-good chemicals. There's also a lot of evidence that what you choose to eat – such as probiotics, less fat, more protein – can increase dopamine production, so maybe look at your diet too. It's helpful to make a list of activities that help you feel safe and good in, and about, your body. Again though, as I'll explain in Principle 7, you'll need to be mindful of your natural tendency to turn whatever feels good into excessive reward.

You may find it helpful to hold in mind **where** most of us say connection with the body is usually found in us and that's our **heart**. Your heart has its own intrinsic nervous system, so when you want to go to a more connected, heart-felt place, try to move your attention down from your head, to your chest and stay there for a while, imagining and breathing into that heart space. Bear in mind that it's also believed that 95 per cent of the feel-good chemical serotonin is actually produced in your gut rather your brain, so maybe also move your attention even lower and take care of that part of you too, whether that's through good diet and nutrition and/or a mindfulness practice that enables you to 'rest and digest' more often.

To maintain balance, you'll need to get to know how your body feels when it's agitated, or numb, and all the ways to gently shift it. You can notice which bodily sensations/feelings you're experiencing that tell you which nervous system is in play. Deep breathing, focusing on long exhales, slowing your heartrate, putting your hand on your heart and breathing into it for a few minutes, sleep, time in the sun and generally spending time outdoors, mindfulness and meditation will all help to introduce and sustain balance. Yoga, stretching, light jogging, laughter, taking care of a pet or children, massage and singing, similarly. Try to make some, or all, of these body-based balancers part of your daily and weekly routines and really notice what you think and feel both before and after doing them.

To help with connection with others, also hold in mind that, although different in shape, your body is something else you have in common with others. Try to avoid comparisons in your head that emphasise difference. Beneath the skin it's all very similar – nobody's blood is blue, black or white.

What you therefore need, and what happens as you establish more balanced connection over time, is for all aspects of your experience to integrate to work together for your common good. All your parts are inextricably bound for life, so you need to encourage them to take each others' hands and take care of each other. But which part of you is internally doing the encouraging? What's pulling the levers to engage your various parts and maintain balanced connection? Which part observes and notes your thoughts, feelings, body and behaviour and then tests, takes the messages from and formulates more helpful responses where needed? This is your guide and I explore this next.

mindfulness

meditation

therapy

counselling

coaching

self-development

5 Invest in
YOUR GUIDE

CHAPTER 10

Principle 5: Invest in Your Guide

As you know, there's no switch to turn off excessive threat/ reward – there are no magic pills – and so balanced connection needs to be coordinated by some part of you. I call this part your 'guide'. I don't believe a dominant guide is something you're born with. It needs to be modelled by others during childhood and adolescence and, as you've seen above, yours may have been given less energy than it needed during these years.

Your guide is the filtering system that stands firmly between your three parts and your internal and external worlds. It's the part of you that notices which of threat/reward/connection you're in at any point in time and makes the decision as to whether or not it's helpful. If and when it decides engagement of a part will cause more trouble than it's worth, it'll warmly, firmly, assure it that it can stand down in favour of another more helpful part. If your guide notices connection, it'll most likely try to enhance it, unless it decides who, or what, you're connecting to would, on balance, not be in your best interests. It decides whether you avoid (threat), approach (reward) and/or attach (connect), always trying to balance your nervous system in the process, so that you are feeling **both** calm (not overly aroused) **and** alive (not under-aroused).

With your guide in control, you hold all the power to make yourself happy: what happens inside you happens **your** way. It reflects on what you're doing before, during and after, and decides when to control and when to let go. You could also see your guide as your emotional processor, amygdala whisperer, observing self, affect regulator, the part of you that buffers as you're buffeted by life or your centre.

The principles you've read about so far are really all about developing and empowering your guide. For you to explore the issues in Principles 1–4, your guide must be present: its existence is implicit in their practice, whether it's taking responsibility by looking at your role in an argument or noticing what you think, believe and feel in your body. Now you've been investing some thought, feeling and behavioural energy into it, it's helpful to be clearer at this point around what your guide needs to maintain balanced connection. To do this, your guide must know how to:

- **Manage your attention**: as you know, threat/reward are naturally automatically outward-looking. To move to balanced connection, you need to be consistently aware of what's happening **inside** you, **before** you respond to external situations. You must be as familiar with your internal landscape as you are with your external. Where the direction of your attention in threat/reward is **outward-in and then up** to threat/reward fantasy, your attention in balanced connection goes **inward and downwards before you, possibly, then go out to act**. Your guide therefore needs to bring your internal experience (thoughts, feelings and body) at any point in time to the forefront of your awareness. You also need to be able to manage your attention from your biases to a more expansive view of yourself and the world.

- Bring you more into contact with **the 'here and now' present moment** to avoid unhelpful threat/reward fantasy/memory.

- **Connect you more with your body.** As you know, a key characteristic of too much threat/reward is frequent disconnection from your body, possibly not being able to feel it at all. In balanced connection, you need to be more **in** your body, aware of its sensations and its innate rhythm and intelligence.

- **Allow you more internal and external silence, so you can be more receptive and stop and listen** more easily to yourself and others.

- **Balance your nervous system.** Only with a balanced nervous system, can you manage threat/reward impulses, feel alive and have the space and freedom to build helpful, balanced connection alternatives.

Two of the most effective 'structured' practices to build your guide are mindfulness/meditation and therapy/counselling/coaching.

Mindfulness/Meditation

The difference between mindfulness and meditation probably isn't important for these purposes, so I'll just use the word 'mindfulness' to cover both. Mindfulness is great at building your guide – it's its gold standard, expert, **free** personal trainer, which is why it's everywhere in the world of modern well-being. When your guide can combine the benefits of mindfulness with intentionally managing your parts where necessary, I think you'll find that your well-being will be largely under your control.

For your guide to be able to establish and maintain balanced connection, your being needs to be **quieter**. Try to see slowing down, resting, stopping, being silent and **listening** to yourself **as doing** something – as essential self-care – from this point on. Mindfulness will help you to do this by focussing your awareness on the present moment and plugging you into yourself so you can touch down inside. And don't let threat worry you that slowing down will somehow make you less effective at your job or life generally – the opposite will be true.

From here, your guide can notice the flow of feelings, thoughts and bodily sensations. This gives it the ability to choose which ones you latch onto and which ones you let pass. Over time, you'll be able to see your thought soup, sensations and feelings as just passing pieces of experience and that if you just gently notice them as they flow through, they'll change and be less able to sustain themselves when they're unhelpful to you.

With mindfulness, you'll equip your guide with the knowledge that you don't have to merge with threat/reward as they try to jerk you away from the present moment to other times and other places, into uncomfortable/euphoric memory/ fantasy and stories or arguments in your head. That you don't need to fall with threat or fly with reward. You'll become better able to tolerate distress without fighting with it and enjoy pleas- urable behaviours and substances without addiction to them. Present, but uninvolved if you don't need to be.

As your threat and reward parts quieten, your guide can then help you relax back into your body and the life that's just here. You'll have fewer of your threat and reward needs to control this moment, to struggle against the way things are. It'll be easier to accept what is and, where necessary, allow and receive it, or let go where something's beyond your control. You'll see that the only thing that's real is **this moment** and that it can often be the beginning, middle and end – a soothing, completely satisfying, place of non-striving. Everything else is either all gone, or hasn't happened yet.

This all helps your guide be able to recognise which of your parts are triggered and when your nervous system is out of balance and to interrupt the progression of what's happening, or enhance it, as necessary. As you become more aware of what's happening inside your body and how to change it, you'll then feel safer and be nurturing your greatest asset: internal peace coupled with aliveness.

Mindfulness uses various 'anchors' for your attention, but practices often favour bodily sensations, senses and breath, because these are always present and accessible to you. The basic mindfulness practice of focusing on your breath – slowing and deepening it – of itself engages your parasympathetic nervous system, which is key if too much arousal is your issue. If you breathe easily, you relax and settle your body, because that's how you breathe when you feel safe. In turn, relaxing your body means you breathe easily, slowing your heartrate, turning down threat and calibrating your body to actual levels of safety. With no agitated body to support your threat/reward thoughts and feelings, your thoughts and feelings can calm down – they assume that if your body isn't worried, then you must be safe.

That mindfulness is all done in silence and stillness (aside, possibly, from voice of a guide – see apps such as Insight Timer for great free guides) also gets you more used to the balanced connection preference for **listening** rather than talking and for **being** rather than doing. Reducing the external input of life as often as you can is so important for keeping connected to yourself. These quiet moments with self free you and feed you as you stop in order to start enjoying solitude more.

You might struggle at first to make a consistent mindfulness practice a habit. Too much threat/reward will put sitting in silence **way down** your list of priorities. They'll make it uncomfortable, maybe even painful. Threat will also, of course, tell you you're not doing it properly. Reward will probably think it's boring. But try to put at least a few minutes of mindfulness on top of your daily to-do list.

To make this as easy as possible for you, I suggest you keep it simple and consistent:

- If you notice one threat thought today as it comes, perhaps label it and allow it to go on its way without riding it – you've been mindful.
- If you notice the heat of the sun on parts of your body on a walk outside, rather than pursuing a thought about how unfairly you've been treated/how good that drink would taste, you've been mindful.
- If you sit and listen to sounds inside the room you're in, then move attention to sounds outside, or notice the different smells or temperatures as you walk through a building, or past a parade of shops, you've been mindful.

Other behaviours that are also potentially mindful include eating, cleaning, gardening, making things, drawing and cooking. There are plenty of ways to give your guide the tools it needs.

As I've mentioned, one of the most familiar mindfulness techniques is to focus on your breath. Your breath connects your internal with the external. When threat/reward look to spin you out, focus on your breath and spend a few moments making sure you're breathing gently and calmly. The over-aroused breath of threat/reward tends to be shallow and taken into your upper chest. When you're calm and in balanced connection, you draw your breath deeply and gently into your abdomen, with a soft belly, so make sure that's what's happening. Most of us don't like to let our abdomens soften and expand, but we have to do this in order to relax. Try to focus on the exhale while you place a hand on your lower abdomen to make sure it gently rises and falls. Make your exhale longer than your inhale to help calm you down. Perhaps breathe 3 in and 5 out. And in through the nose and out through the mouth, so you don't hyperventilate.

Make a point of trying to test your ability to change your state in this way whenever you remember – if it's bad traffic, busy streets or waiting in line at the supermarket that arouses your nervous system, that's great because you'll probably have opportunities to practise calming yourself with mindfulness and breath this week. Notice what your body feels like before you try the mindfulness and then what it feels like after. You need to be familiar with the sensations of both a calm and aroused body if you're going to maintain a balanced connection.

Sometimes, you can also just notice your breath untouched and allow yourself to 'be breathed'. Allowing this natural ebb and flow can be a great way to connect to your aliveness when your nervous system is under-aroused. You come to realise you can trust your breath and, implicitly therefore, your body and yourself. It's a great relief for threat/reward to realise the most important act of staying alive happens, that your aliveness exists, without you even trying to control it.

Therapy/Counselling

You can see that the principles so far have mainly been about connecting more with **yourself**. It's unlikely, though, that moving from threat/reward to a more balanced connection can be done by the same threat/reward worldview that created it. For all the 'vicious circle' reasons I've mentioned throughout this book, without external intervention, dominant threat/reward usually tighten the screws over time.

You can use the threat/reward outward-in preference to your advantage though, whether it's with guided audio mindfulness practices and/or mindfulness classes or good counselling and/or psychotherapy. Again, for simplicity, I'll use one word for the latter: 'therapy'. I'm also only really referring to 'talking therapy' below, although there are many other great techniques out there you might want to look into, including drama, art, dance, music therapy etc.

Good therapy can build your guide in lots of ways. It gently directs your attention inwards and encourages curiosity about your internal landscape, allowing you to explore your current ways of being and doing. This way, you can bring your parts and their patterns of thoughts, feelings and behaviours above the radar into more conscious awareness. You can ground the great and the good in you, decide on those aspects that no longer serve you and work out balanced connection alterna- tives. The weekly nature of therapy means you can practise new ways of experiencing yourself and others in the natural cycle of your week.

Something that may put you off therapy which I often hear is there's no point looking back, that we need to move forward and look to the future. However, as you can see from the above, for your guide to establish and maintain balanced connection, you're going to need to rewind and look back, at least initially. **Your past isn't actually past – it determines your present.** You know by now that threat/reward always worry about present 'danger' and/or reward and spend very little time trying to understand who you are, how you got here and where you're going. Without developing this more connected, empathetic and compassionate view of self, you're most likely going to continue with threat's childhood belief that your distress is your own fault.

Through good therapy, you'll see you're made up of every experience you've had to date, as well as many of those in your family tree. You can then place responsibility (not fault or blame) for childhood patterns where they really belong. The only problem with looking back can be when it's coupled with anger and resentment. Good therapy ought to mean that, once you've felt and acknowledged this anger and the reasons for it, you can, over time, let go of it so that it doesn't taint your present anymore.

By turning your experiences into words or images in a safe, confidential and non-judgemental environment, your guide will have the benefit of a de-shaming, coherent narrative about what has happened to you, who you are and where you're going. It's not necessarily the degree of distress you've experienced that determines how unhappy you are now, it's the extent to which you've formed a balanced, connected and compassionate narrative about what happened and the effect it's had on you.

Leading on from really knowing you're not responsible for what happened to you in early experience, good therapy helps your guide take full responsibility for yourself now. You'll need to bear in mind threat/reward's capacity, often imperative, to lie to you, engage in delusional self-talk or be overly harsh/lenient on you. Therapy should help you to see how this might be playing out in your life and to work out more helpful options.

That good therapy provides a safe place characterised by confidentiality, a non-judgemental approach, compassion, patience, honesty and courage should also mean your connection to and trust in others grows. You can put the previously unsayable into words that are heard by another without the shaming that threat engages in. Unlike caregivers controlled by threat/reward, a good therapist should have no unconscious vested interest in you remaining the same, or possibly even changing in a particular way. As you find this a rewarding experience, your increased trust in others takes with it your trust in yourself, and your own guide.

For all the essential ways that therapy is necessarily different from other relationships, it's also two human beings relating to each other. Whatever happens for you outside of the therapy room in relationships is therefore likely to happen inside. If you tend to want others to always take care of you and hand over your power in this way, you'll probably do this with your therapist. If you have problems with boundaries (see Principle 9), this usually gets acted out. If you believe people take you for granted or undervalue you, again, you're likely to feel this in the therapeutic relationship. If you talk about it, this can all be worked through in a safe and non-shaming space.

Specific threat/reward beliefs can also be looked at in therapy, including that:

- Focusing attention on yourself is 'selfish/self-indulgent'. Balanced connection reframes this as essential self-care.

- Therapy will make you dependent. At least a short- to medium-term experience of dependency may even be what you need for a while. If you've lost some control over yourself, let someone trustworthy help you with the wheel initially. Of course, long-term therapy dependency is in no one's best interests, but in my experience, this isn't what happens.

- 'Feeling better' is not happening fast enough. You need to accept that the process of internalising what therapy provides, and bringing it into life, takes time. The wounds you're healing were often made a long time ago. The healing process takes time too, so try to be patient. Patience is a quality of balanced connection.

Finding the right therapist for you

I talk about **good** therapy above to distinguish it from any therapy. All therapy training, all therapists and all clients are different. There's a wide range in what clients will therefore experience within generally accepted therapeutic boundaries. So how do you know what kind of therapy, or therapist, is right for you?

If some, or all, of these principles ring true for you, it might be helpful to think about how you'll work on them in therapy, bearing in mind the inevitable threat distortions and biases. As with all of us, some therapists may also not be managing their own parts as well as they might. You'll hopefully notice this when you're with them. Perhaps look at the therapist and decide whether this is how you'd like to be and relate to others. If you notice a pattern of threat feelings, or even too much connection, try to talk about it. And, if this doesn't result in you feeling more comfortable, then do consider leaving.

Something else to bear in mind is that talking about problems amplifies them in your awareness with your biases. Therapy might therefore **wire in** more attention to pain and distress. Of course you need to talk about your pain and for it to be felt and experienced in therapy, for all the reasons mentioned above. But if this is all that ever happens, if you seem to be going round the same narrow threat/reward loops and/or only ever really talking about other people, you might be ingraining the pain more deeply. So be mindful of this. As well as problems, flaws and distress, try to spend time grounding and cultivating your resources. As ever, you need **balance** here.

6 Use your
CREATIVE IMAGINATION

CHAPTER 11

Principle 6: Use Your Creative Imagination

When threat/reward dominate, you're probably not spending much time thinking creatively about your future. Your threat thoughts are mental contractions: unconsciously believing you're about to die is not the place of imagining what the world has to offer, or what you have to offer it. Threat has an inbuilt **inability** to build an appealing future and can make your imagination your own worst enemy. Excessive reward is just as unhelpful, with its repetitive, short-termist, one-dimensional fantasies. Your imagination, and what you use it for, is therefore a key way for your guide to maintain a balanced connection.

You know that brains similar to yours reached the moon, established complex systems of health and social care to take care of each other, built the iPhone and Paris, wrote the Prince catalogue and animated Avatar. Your imagination has this same capacity for greatness: an endless, timeless and vast creative resource, that's unrestricted by your physical body or your situation in life. A resource that's just yours. Combine this with the letting go of limiting beliefs/values and you can live a life full of interest, meaning and purpose, using your imagination as a powerful resource for your guide to keep your parts in balance and shape your future.

Because you live through your brain's imagery, **you can change your world by changing how you imagine it**. You need your guide to be making sure your imagination works for you rather than against you, creating the peace or stimulation you might have in the past believed can only come from reward behaviours and substances. Your guide must now use your imagination to create images and fantasies that produce and enhance the connection feelings, giving you the forward-moving energy needed for connected, creative behaviours.

There are so many ways you can develop your creative imagination for these purposes: writing, art, singing, playing music, dance, garden design, starting a business, loving gestures, redecorating a room, doodling, creating a menu for dinner for friends, working out a holiday itinerary, messaging someone some words of appreciation, putting together an exercise plan, flower arrangement, working out what you're wearing tomorrow, making sushi, writing computer code, designing an app… to name just a few.

Another structured way to engage your creative imagination is making a 'vision' or 'dream board'. Just take a cork or poster board, along with magazines you can cut photos and quotes from, and, using scissors, pins, tape and/or glue, attach to your board any of those images, quotes and destinations that **resonate with, inspire and motivate** you. It can be helpful to hold particular areas in mind, such as relationships, career, physical health, finances and personal development while you're doing it. Try to give yourself at least an hour to put it together and bear in mind there aren't any rules – there are no right or wrong boards. As well as helping you to construct a future, you know that whatever you give your attention to grows and that the neural pathways activated when you imagine doing something are the same as when you actually do them, so creating a board like this can be a really effective way to connect more with yourself, your environment and your future.

However you do it, you need to try to connect with and imagine the future you want and that you're working towards now. A future that's worth doing all of this for; a future worth **living** for. Excessive threat/reward have been imagining scenarios all the time anyway, just featuring mostly unseen enemies, pints of lager and new cars. Try to imagine what your ideal day would look like from start to finish and, as always, make it detailed. What would it look, sound, smell, taste and feel like?

If you create, and believe in, a loving, fulfilling, energising future, your guide will be able to ensure that's what comes to pass. In fact, if you imagine it in this moment, in a way you're already there aren't you? Dominant threat/reward might tell you it's deluded, but, as always, just nod compassionately at them and manage your attention back to connection.

Three other simple creative imagination resources you can use are:

1. Your safe, calm or peaceful place. Imagine this place in as much detail as possible: what it looks, sounds, smells, tastes and feels like. Try to avoid having other people there, because they can come with unconscious, dysregulating consequences. As you imagine this place, notice the change in your physiological state as your nervous system moves more into balance. Installing it, as ever, by expanding the experience throughout your body for as long as you can. And then repeat this whenever you can.

2. A moment in the past you felt confident, competent and connected to yourself and others. It can be from any time in your life and in any situation. And if it's not straightaway to hand, keep digging, because you'll find it. Again, connect to this moment with all your senses, expand and embody it and bring it to mind and body as often as you can remember.

3. Your loved one. Simply imagine a particular moment looking at the person you love most in this world. This is what love **looks like**. Keep imagining them whenever you can and, as ever, notice the effect this has on your feelings/body.

You can see that you'll be working on the balanced connection aim of feeling both calm and alive with the imagination resources I've described above: the peaceful place and loved one taking care of calm and the ideal future, loved one and confident/competent moments also stimulating your aliveness.

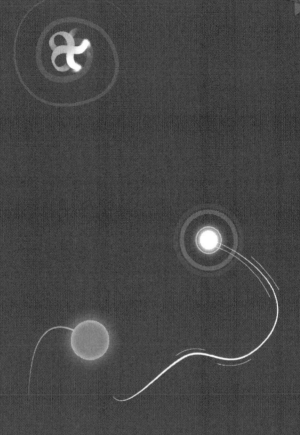

7 Enjoy
YOURSELF

CHAPTER 12

Principle 7: Enjoy Yourself

Carrying on with the idea of crowding too much threat/ reward out, an effective and enjoyable way to do this is to use reward **in a measured, balanced and skilful way** to naturally provide you with feel-good chemicals.

Dominant threat/reward both have problems with reward. As you know, pure threat is the place of under- or over-arousal, stress hormones, lacking the means to make you feel good, except maybe for the relief you feel as you avoid the imagined/ real threat. Excessive reward is the place of feel-good chemicals, but having either too much, or too few, of them. They're its answer to everything – highs or lows. If threat is too dominant, your guide therefore needs to increase your levels of feel-good chemicals. If you're controlled by reward, it's got to learn to water them down so they're not the sole reason for your existence.

Your guide can deliberately encourage the production of feel-good chemicals with your mind, body and behaviour. As you've seen above with thoughts, creative imagination will naturally produce them. In terms of the body and behaviours, connected human touch, such as massage, sex, holding hands and hugs, and other behaviours like sleep, completing goals/ missions/quests, mindfulness, dancing, drinking water, smiling and laughing, running, warm showers, very cold showers, a walk in the park, singing lullabies, stroking a pet, applying hand cream and healthy eating will all do the same. Start noticing the many ways you can produce feel-good chemicals **naturally**. As well as your own ideas, you might look to others for inspiration. What gives each of us pleasure may differ – from looking at vintage cars, to going to comedy clubs, to rom coms, to dressing up as a solider and recreating historical battles on Sundays, it's all up to you now. So keep your own list somewhere, add to it and draw from it when necessary. Very simply, from this point

141

on, each day, **try to do more of what makes you happy**. Even put a couple of enjoyable events in your diary now and make them regular weekly ones if possible.

As ever, you'll be managing threat and/or reward along your way, with unhelpful threat's familiar limiting beliefs that you won't enjoy something and/or you're not the sort of person who can do it and/or reward wanting too much of the feel-good chemicals. To manage the self-doubt, you know you'll need to try to fake it to make it sometimes and to go ahead despite feeling some anxiety with new experiences. If you do something threat told you you couldn't, or shouldn't, do, the probability is it'll work out well. You'll then get the natural reward from doing it, encouraging you to do it again. Just try whatever it is a few times and see what it actually **feels like** in your body. It may, of course, not be your thing – that's fine, as long as that's not based on excessive threat, and as long as you're using your creative imagination to think of alternatives.

You also need to bear in mind reward's well-intentioned, but potentially destructive, short-termism. As we saw above, lots of behaviours and substances that trigger reward can hijack your whole being. You could fill your list of feel-good activities with the big addictive substances and behaviours. In fact, your current list may be made up of some or all of these. But you know that if that's **all** you do, it may end badly for you.

Your guide needs to distinguish between helpful mood-managing reward and where reward is talking you into carrying on in an unhealthy, possibly terminal, relationship with a substance and/or behaviour. Trick or treat? You must know which one's which. You may even need others, such as a therapist, to help you tell the difference. Constantly taking in chemicals or engaging in behaviours that flood your brain with so much dopamine that your dopamine receptors die off, meaning you can no longer enjoy just relaxing, a warm day or birdsong, is not your guide's idea of a good time.

One of the main problems with being controlled by reward is that it makes it more difficult for you to enjoy life's simple pleasures. You lose the capacity to be **truly content and satisfied** with just being or doing ordinary things. Reward becomes a one- or two-trick pony, as it gets enjoyment/connection and short-term intensity confused. Like, for example, thinking sex is love – although someone might look, even feel, like they love you when they're having, or want to have, sex with you and vice versa, sex is not love and love is not sex. Excessive reward believes fun is about **intense** experiences, experiences that are often not **enjoyable** felt experiences in the round. If you 'can't' enjoy a walk in the sunshine, coffee with friends, petting a dog, smelling the roses, watching a film you love, drinking a glass of water, resting, looking at the clouds pass, a hug, dancing, a good memory, laughing, sleeping, reading a new book, exercising or eating a good meal, then reward may have been hijacked already. Your guide is going to need to oversee its reconditioning and recalibration from this point on as part of your move to balanced connection.

In my experience, when reward is too controlling it may actually take longer to shift than too much threat because, whereas turning threat down and turning connection up usually feels good, turning reward down, at least in the short term, often hurts with the resulting cravings and frustration. But, although new sources of gentle, natural feel-good chemicals will not be as quick to move you to connection and aliveness as crystal meth or buying yet another expensive gift for yourself on your credit card, no one ever lost their friends and family, their health and/ or their financial security because they petted a dog too much, laughed all afternoon with friends or felt really relaxed during mindfulness.

So as well as making it more difficult for reward to dominate (for example, parental controls on phones and computers if your issue is a sex or gambling addiction) and turning down the threat that's often the fuel for addiction, your guide needs to ensure that you're most often in connection instead and doing interesting, pleasurable things in life that you can't do when you're controlled by reward. Try to **balance** fun, pleasure, entertainment and reward with silence, relaxation and peace: again balancing calmness and aliveness. You'll find calmness will become rewarding over time, as you turn threat/reward down. You'll notice that the best things in life really are free. That's not to say, of course, that the usual addiction behaviours and substances shouldn't be on your list –

some good food, buying new things and good sex will often be part of a balanced connection life.

It's worth noting that film, music and social media are likely to be on your feel-good list. They can be great ways to reward yourself and relax. Try to notice, though, whether reward and relaxation **is** the effect they're having. Music, film and other media can often be promoting and sustaining unhelpful threat/reward. A diet of media or video games containing violence, threat, aggression and horror, will all be pressing your threat button. And we all know the predominance in the media of sex, money, drugs, novelty, competition, gambling, and so on, in terms of sustaining reward.

As for social media, although when in balanced connection, you'll be able to make sure it's just used to connect with others and is therefore a helpful tool, if threat/reward are too dominant, you're likely to use it to sustain them. The outwards-in, comparisons, reactive anger and narcissistic characteristics of threat, for example, can be fed by lots of social media use. At least at first therefore, you probably need to be spending less time on social media, to give yourself more breathing space and time for self-reflection.

Your guide needs to be aware that you are what you actually and metaphorically eat. Everything you take into your body through your mouth, ears and eyes, is mind- and emotion-/body-affecting. Everything will release chemicals/engage one of your parts. Try to notice what's happening from a feeling/bodily point of view when you play that computer game, watch that film, check Instagram or even read the news. You know that threat and reward are the parts that will most easily run away with your attention, which is why the news is full of things you 'should' be frightened of and/or angry about and/or stimulated by. The media is largely about getting your attention, especially in today's hypercompetitive, clickbait environment. You may therefore need to be really discriminating about the media you choose to expose yourself to.

It's also worth bearing in mind that even music, TV, films, computer games, social media and books that move you into connection are all outward-in ways to do it. Although you choose whatever it is, you're then a passive recipient. This is all good, as long as you're also balancing this with working towards connection using inward focus and awareness and management of your attention. You need to be able to shift yourself to connection without always relying on outside input. You also need to balance these more passive behaviours with ones that involve **movement, action and active interaction, both alone and with others**.

Just in terms of adjusting brain chemicals, I think antide-pressant and anti-anxiety medication can sometimes be helpful for your guide in the short-term. Excessive threat/reward tighten up so much through their self-fulfilling prophecies that they can leave no room for you to breathe, no safe distance from which you can notice, reflect and therefore choose. Please bear in mind though, that if nothing other than taking a daily pill changes over time, it's possible that once you stop taking it, your internal and external landscapes will, over time, move you back to living in too much threat/reward. You might therefore need medi-cation initially to help your guide do its job, but do also work on these principles to enable the sustainable, long-term shift in experience you're probably wanting here. **Medication just can't compensate, long-term, for a lack of connection.**

8 Connect
WITH OTHERS

CHAPTER 13

Principle 8: Connect with Others

Palliative-care doctor Ira Byock, who worked with the dying, wrote in his book *The Four Things That Matter Most* that when we're dying, what we want to do is tell people we love them, ask them for forgiveness, tell them we forgive them and say thank you to them. All the connection things we should have said, but we didn't say; all the connection things we should have done, but we didn't do. Presumably no one preoccupies about possessions, status or appearance on their death bed. At no point does anyone raise their head from the pillow to whisper to their relatives 'Get rich or die tryin'', 'Do I look fat in this?' or even 'Yay, I won.'

I think the dying must have their priorities right. They face the root of all fear and it's **real** this time. Notice that what gives them peace, contentment and reward are the **connection behaviours** of **expressing** love, gratitude and forgiveness. And that these are the most difficult things to say, even think and feel, about self and others during a life driven by threat/reward.

I've spent much of this book looking at initiating and sustaining a balanced connection relationship with self. Now it's time to look at relationships with others. With a better-established balanced connection relationship with yourself, good relationships with other people are another key way to live a balanced connection life.

The effect of dominant threat/reward on relationships with others

As you know, too much threat/reward are your connection dam, harming relationships with others in the way they do your relationship with self. When threat is too dominant, your experience of other people can be characterised by much more fear/anger than is helpful or necessary for you.

As you know, when threat is triggered more than it needs to be (and social interactions will be one of those places where, by and large, it just doesn't need to be unless you socialise with sociopaths), it'll compromise your ability to regulate yourself and/or help regulate others. You might therefore often lack the willingness, or even ability, to repair relationships so fundamental to balanced connection with yourself and your environment, having little confidence that threat can be managed in relationships with others. You may therefore be spending far too much energy on either breaking relationships or fixing them.

Time and again, threat may have meant that getting close to people means you getting hurt. In short, you might think people can be 'hell' and have become good at leaving them based on unhelpful threat's false promise of protection. And this increased isolation, in turn, leaves you without the information other people can actually provide to counter unhelpful threat/reward beliefs about yourself and the world around you.

Excessive reward can also mean, without knowing it, that others are treated just as a means to a rewarding end, rather than as human ends in themselves. The secrets, lies and lack of integrity and empathy around at times in addictions can further disconnect you.

As you know, when threat dominates, you might relate to other people in terms of inferiority/superiority; putting yourself down in your own mind in relation to them or putting them down to inflate you. Reward might also be fuelling comparisons, as you get the high of 'winning' in your imagination. Whatever the reason and whichever way you cut it, comparisons are disconnecting and really can steal your joy. Most of what you have, and who you are, is unseen in these moments of comparison. You might also choose to be around people because of what they look like, their status or what they have, rather than who they are, therefore feeding unhelpful threat/reward.

Of course, it's human nature to compare and comparisons are encouraged all the time in today's society. Facebook,

Instagram and Snapchat all feature images, usually capturing the 'best' of people's lives – a 'spontaneous' moment where everything can be made to look just 'perfect', notwithstanding it was the fifteenth take and is processed through a vivid warm filter. Advertisers often **intend** to provoke comparison by creating a viewing experience outside of most human reality to encourage you to spend your money. If you came off better in the comparison, you'd have no incentive to buy. But there's no way you, as a beautifully imperfect human being, can consistently compare to the technology-enhanced, idealised product of someone else's imagination.

Because of the toxic duo of an often outward-in focus and lack of a grounded sense of your own worth, threat can couple a pervasive belief that others can't be trusted, with being too dependent on their input. It will struggle to expect support from others. It might tell you that you shouldn't expect to feel better as a result of relationships, and somewhere holds the belief that you're going to be mistreated, exploited and manipulated. But it equally wants the external validation, giving others too much responsibility for and power over your well-being. You might preoccupy about other people 'disrespecting' you in this place.

One of the reasons you might struggle to trust others when you are driven by threat/reward is that you can struggle with being trustworthy yourself. Maybe you give up secrets/confidences to show you've been confided in, showing lack of empathy, integrity and boundaries. If it's difficult at times to trust yourself to hold boundaries and contain information, it's understandable you'll believe others will find this difficult too. But these behaviours make relationships less safe and therefore compromise your ability to maintain connection.

You might also often be worried about what others think and feel about you and, with threat's biases, assume there's a problem. As you know, there are important balanced connection reasons for your guide to be interested in what other people think about you. Being able to notice whether or not someone likes you is important in taking care of yourself and others. As you also know, though, threat often pushes you out to guessing, predicting and 'knowing' the operation of other people's minds. It will always interpret them as threatening, amplifying and

149

sensitising you to slights from imagined enemies, overlooking all of those times when interactions were either neutral or enjoyable, and negating all the past goodwill.

When threat is too dominant, you might also think about the ideas of 'normal' and 'weird' and even use them against connection's preference for expressing your true nature. Again, an awareness of, and some compliance with, social norms and conventions is important for your guide to maintain balanced connection with others. But being driven by threat will mean you worry too much about whether you're 'normal' in this way or 'weird' in that way, as if there are invisible, pervasive, enforced social laws sitting miles outside of your control. As a result, you might believe you have no choice but to obey them, disconnected from yourself and the wider world as you get angry with 'them' about it. When really all 'they' are probably doing is getting on with their own business today. Unhelpful threat would be in for quite a disappointment if it knew how little others actually think about you.

I think 'people-pleasing' can get a lot of bad press. Your guide knows that to please people initiates and sustains healthy relationships and feels good for you too. Too much reliance on threat, though, may mean that you have a tendency to need **everyone** to like you, which might too often mean putting pleasing others **above** pleasing yourself. If you think too much about pleasing other people, you might forget to live your own connected life.

This urge to always please others may also be compounded by a struggle for self-worth, to even know you exist, except through the eyes of another person. You might not therefore be yourself when you relate to others for fear that they won't like what they see. Why would they if you don't? And if you're not relaxed with others, it reduces the potential for intimacy and, with it, the reward you'd otherwise get from an intimate, connected relationship. As you know, if you have a distorted perception of self, it means you won't have put much thought into who you really are and who the other person is actually therefore relating to.

When threat/reward are too dominant, you might also keep people in your life who really shouldn't be there. Reward can maintain connections with other people because they abuse substance and/or behaviours too. Excessive threat's under-arousal and/or submissiveness and familiarity with the victim/perpetrator/rescuer triangle might lead you to sometimes continue powerlessly in unhealthy dynamics, particularly with the unconscious caregivers of parents, partners, even children. Threat/reward's lack of self-esteem means you won't often think you deserve better, and their biases lead you to believe there's nothing better out there anyway.

Because of its lack of trust, fear of confrontation and often analysing other's behaviour, threat might also mean you too often talk **about** others rather than **to** them. You may remain in relationships with people who you spend most of your time criticising behind their back, possibly for good reason, rather than voicing your feelings and concerns in a way that **could** make a difference to their behaviour. In more reflective moments, you may notice you can be 'two-faced' or 'bitchy' for this reason. Further, dominant threat/reward's outward-in preoccupation, their lack of empathy and grounded sense of your own worth and their reluctance to take responsibility, might also mean you focus much less on your impact **on** others, than the other way around.

So, the lack of depth and intimacy in relationships, combined with threat behaviours, superiority and/or inferiority complexes, lack of trust, integrity and empathy, a fear of assertion of rights and opinions, the victim/perpetrator/rescuer triangle, some inflexibility, rigidity and unpredictability, to name just a few, can all mean truly supportive, nurturing balanced connection relationships are few and far between when threat/reward are in control.

You can see how too much threat/reward have a tendency to cut you off from one of your greatest potential sources of safety, connection and reward in life: **other people**. You've evolved to feel happier around others – good social relation-ships **balance** your nervous system. You need to bear in mind then that **if you disconnect from the larger group, which can be dominant threat's tendency, you disconnect from a key way for you to heal**.

Moving to balanced connection with others

In terms of overarching beliefs, try to hold in mind that it's **a basic need** of yours to have deep and intimate relationships in your life. Expect and believe that you deserve to get a healthy proportion of your emotional needs met through a balanced combination of intimate connections with yourself, other people and your community. That other people's beauty helps you to find and sustain connection with your own.

Try whenever you can to work towards getting love, support and help from others and returning the favour. So that relationships are experienced mostly as a treat, as quality time. Although in more balanced connection it's likely you'll have more relationships than when driven by threat, it's not a numbers game, despite social media's obsession with 'likes' and 'followers'. It's the **quality of the relationships and dynamics** that you want to be conscious of. You really just need to be loved by, and love, a few good people.

And if you don't buy all this now, you may need to do some faking it to make it. If you get threat thoughts and feelings in response to a coffee invitation, try to breathe and go anyway. Despite doubts, do reach out, initiate contact with and invest time and effort in others, including new people – perhaps one new person every few weeks; whatever is practical for you.

To increase connection with others, focus on growing intimacy in your relationships by trusting others enough to show more of yourself than dominant threat/reward have allowed in the past. Try to be more open and honest about your thoughts and feelings, although always under the direction of your guide. You'll then have something much closer to real connection with people, as they relate to a more complete version of you and not an overly controlled one that is dictated by threat/reward.

Of course, in terms of balance, your guide needs to discriminate between who to invest in using some helpful threat. The guy who reduces others to tears with his 'bantz' probably isn't ever the best choice. Some gentle teasing can be fun, and perhaps even shows feeling secure and trust in others, but bear in mind that people dictated by threat might use 'banter' to express anger, demean, hurt and bully. And packaging it in humour means they can just accuse you of being over-sensitive if you understandably don't like it, rather than take responsibility for their unhelpful threat behaviour. Of course banter won't kill you, but we're talking about getting a sense of happiness and well-being through connection with others here, not just surviving.

Have a think about who is in your life at the moment. What are those relationship dynamics like in light of what you know now? Are they adult-to-adult, for example, or are there some unhelpful hidden parent/child dynamics operating below the radar? What do you feel like in your body when you're around each of them? If you often drink alcohol when you're around certain people, are you sure it's really them you like and not the effects of the alcohol? Are the people you're around largely supportive and generally regulate themselves well? From this point on, maybe try to prioritise relationships with people who you **genuinely like** and around whom you tend to feel warm, connected and safe. Excessive threat may keep people in your life just because they're rich, hot or well-connected, or because you're afraid of what would happen if you moved them out of it. And the same vice versa. Too much reward may keep them there because they are loaded/get loaded. These may also, of course, be great, connected people, but try to be conscious of what you're feeling, and why, when you're around them.

When you know more about who you are and what you want and need, over time you'll find your tribe or community of like-minded people. That doesn't mean there isn't room in your life for the drama queens and kings and generous, charismatic, narcissistic hosts. Some reward is needed to add fun, intensity and colour to a balanced connection life. But, in balanced connection, these people can be an option rather than your priority.

As for threat's tendency to take people-pleasing too far, maybe think about the 'rule of ten', i.e. with nine other strangers in a room at a party, three will like you, three won't mind either way and three may dislike you. It isn't possible to be every-one's cup of tea and that's fine – you can still be safe, fulfilled and happy. Try to let go of the need to be liked by everyone in order to reduce imagined threat, if this is what you experience.

When you're trying to be liked all the time, you're also focusing completely on the other person, rather than dropping inside and checking whether you actually like them.

Bear in mind that you can't ever fully know, or change, the life experiences that largely decide what someone else thinks about you. And that can turn on whether it's a sunny day or how much beer they've drunk, both of which are, again, completely outside of your control. If the other person's threat is triggered, you might go from hero to zero in seconds. It doesn't mean you're either.

In balanced connection, being less outward-in means you're less inclined to stand or fall on another person's opinion of you. Of course, if people give you compliments, try to accept, be grateful for, expand and embody them rather than cringing away, but your value and worth shouldn't lessen because someone else struggles to see it or be dependent on another putting you up on a pedestal. A bit of adulation and acclaim is all good, deserved and necessary at times for you, but crowns can come with unreasonable, limiting expectations of a human being that you may neither want, nor need, now.

Often, whether someone likes you or not, says more about them than it does about you. Others are in the shape of their past as much as you are. When you relate to anyone, you also relate to their biases – the best and worst (often the worst as you now know) of their experiences, family system, teachers, etc. and who and whatever else significantly affected them. Without awareness and conscious self-management, what they think about you is mainly determined by this material, as it is the other way around. When they're being mean to you, maybe they're unconsciously hoping someone else from their past, or even their present, is feeling the pain you might experience as a result.

How you see yourself is far more important than how others see you and you therefore need to have your own balanced, connected, grounded sense of who you are. As long as you're comfortable that you're most often acting in accordance with connection qualities, such as integrity, equanimity, patience and respect, taking responsibility and apologising and making amends where needed, try to allow yourself just to get on with your life and let other people process their response to it.

Know that second-guessing what others **think** about you is mostly a waste of your precious thoughts and feelings. As Mother Theresa suggested, maybe even think of it as **none of your business** if that's helpful for you. Of course if you polled 100 people on the question of whether you're charming and successful and 98 of them tick both boxes, it could suggest some objective truth. But what dominant threat believes other people think about you isn't ever based on formal polling (and actually, we know how unreliable even that can be). It's most often just unreliable fantasy. The less time you spend trying to control mostly fictional, largely random and always invisible thoughts of others, the more you have to spend on your own happiness – on your own balanced connection.

Of course it's important not to disregard others if you're to maintain connections. You need to listen to their expressed view on you (and that means **explicitly** expressed, not just that someone 'looked at me funny' or took a day to respond on WhatsApp even though there were two ticks and they had definitely therefore read the message). Take some space and see if you think it's true. If it is, on some level you may know it already anyway. You might then choose to change your behaviour, if you believe there's a good reason to do so to keep connected. Keeping your guide in charge of your relationships internally and externally is all you can control, is the best you can do and therefore has to be good enough.

It might be that you decide, based on someone's patterns of behaviour, that it's best that they shouldn't be in your life any more (see page 161 for more on this). Often, though, try to navigate threat's rocky times and move on in relationships despite them, and, where you need to, suggest changes to reflect your (balanced connection) feelings. Even balanced connection relationships will have their threat moments, but hold onto the fact that they are worth saving in spite of this. Try to be mindful of threat's need to be right and to win. Other people most often say and do unhelpful things for the same reason you do – not managing their parts as well as they might and because they weren't shown how to often enough. And they do things differently from you just, well, **because they aren't you**.

You may therefore need to **yield** sometimes where it's in the best interests of maintaining a relationship. In fact, you might see your capacity to yield at times as a strength. Threat anger will want you to make the other person bend the knee in an argument for the high of winning, but it just isn't worth it for you in the medium- to long-term with people who you want in your life, for life. They might just take their revenge on you out of your sight in some other way anyway by, for example, having an affair in a romantic relationship or talking about you behind your back and betraying confidences in a friendship. Your world won't cave in if you bend, so try to hold in mind trust, forgiveness and patience, and empathise where you can with the other person's position. You know excessive threat has got it twisted if you'll apologise to a stranger who bumps into you, but not to your partner for calling them an arsehole.

Try to make a conscious effort to soothe, comfort and regulate yourself when you're hurt in relationships to reduce your tendency to react with threat behaviours. Bear in mind the difference between the balanced connection behaviour of calmly, verbally **defending** yourself and the threat behaviour of verbally **attacking** another person. If someone is regularly putting you down, to tell them that when they say those things you feel hurt and you'd like them to stop it, is defending yourself. To get angry and call them a 'bitch' is verbally attacking them.

Another key way to increase connection in relationships is to help and take care of other people and to accept their help and care where you can. In neuroscientific terms, caring for someone activates connection in the way that being cared for does. Being selfless makes **you** feel good too. Where threat believes you'll 'burden' others if you go to them for help, know instead that accepting others' kindness, support and generosity most often helps them to feel good too. It's a win–win. Also, try to honour and celebrate the **value** of other people to you whenever you can. Whether that's through remembering their birthday, saying thank you and/or thinking about what's happening in their lives and actively letting them know you're doing this.

In terms of this care for others, do be mindful of too much threat possibly leading you to care-take at the expense of your own needs. When caring for others, always bear in mind that your primary responsibility is to take care of yourself. The key, as ever, is balance. How do you make sure you're not 'pathologically' caretaking? In balanced connection you help and give because you feel good when you do it. You're most often fulfilled by it rather than always depleted and it doesn't usually go hand in hand with resentment that someone isn't doing the same back.

Also hold in mind that you aren't **responsible** for another adult's happiness. And vice versa. Take care of them, support them, love them, listen to and be there for them, advise them if they ask you to, get help for them if you're really worried about them, but know it's not your **responsibility** that someone else is controlled by threat/reward and it's impossible for you to move them to balanced connection anyway. You're only responsible for your own happiness and that of your real dependants – your children and pets (and, by the way, be mindful too of believing, below the radar, that any children you may have are responsible for **your** happiness). Of course, it's great to offer helpful knowledge, advice and support to others in distress and these might catch within them over time. But what another sane, grown adult does with their lives is really their business and their choice, no matter their relationship to you and/or how distressing their choices might be for you. All that's within your control is whether to accept them, try to change the dynamic (through clear communication of your needs and wants and/or changing yourself) or to see less of them, or even not at all if need be.

Another way of connecting more with people is to try to **see yourself in others and others in yourself**. We're all much more similar than we are different – we mostly all meet our needs for safety, reward and connection in that order and often get stuck bouncing around between the first two. We all cry, can create and destroy, need to love and be loved, get frightened and angry. **Every** person in **every** room you go into has struggled in the way you do and has the same capacity for love, happiness and creativity that you do. Irrespective of race, gender, culture or sexuality, you can connect to anyone by means of a basic, imperfect and beautiful humanity. An old Metta Loving Kindness prayer you can say in your head when you're struggling to connect with another person is: 'May you be well, may you be happy, may you be satisfied', or something similar.

Generally, after the initial, inevitable threat comparisons do your best to be happy for other people when things go well for them. Try to **avoid comparing yourself to others. Instead, only compare you to you in the past** and, again, direct most of your attention to taking care of your own business. As you know, it's important to be mindful of and moderate any tendency you might have to compare and compete all the time with other people. Some competition is enjoyable and motivating for you, but **always competing is always being disconnected**. You need balance, with the emphasis on connection, as ever.

When interacting with others, try to let them have their own felt experience, without threat personalising their unhappiness and thinking it's because of you. We're all entitled to be unhappy at times, including you of course, even though the timing may be inconvenient for someone else. Another person having their own separate felt experience is not somehow threatening. Try to move away from dominant threat messages that someone has to 'put a smile' on their face, or pull themselves together, for you, and vice versa. If they don't want to share why they're unhappy, maybe just leave them to it, take care of making yourself happy and trust they'll most often regulate themselves in due course. Try to steer away from expecting 'perfection' in others, because, as we know, perfection is excessive threat fiction. Accept their differences and flaws, like you want them to accept yours, always being mindful of your threat biases. This is, of course, subject to addressing any ongoing pattern of poor behaviour.

By modelling balanced connection in your own life, **you both show other people how to treat you and make it easy for them to love you**. Ask yourself why others should love you. If you try to be loving and lovable, the result is often that you'll get the love you want from others. And if you don't, at least you'll know you did what you could and maintained your own self-respect and dignity if you leave. For all relationships, and importantly romantic ones, as hard as I know it can be, try to hold in mind now that friendships, hugs and kisses **aren't legally binding**. People change over time, so try at some point to let go of any resentment and anger if someone chooses to no longer be in a relationship with you. No one's yours to keep, including children. You can, and I'm sure will be, loving and lovable enough that good people will want to be around you for your lifetime.

To make sure people do stay around and you keep connected, try to treat your partner, parents, friends and children with at least the same respect as you would a stranger. You don't need to buy that 'All couples fight' and 'We argue because we love each other so much.' You argue and fight when you feel hurt and/or threatened and struggle to control your anger. If you want to remain connected, to really love and be loved, try to be conscious of your behaviour towards those you say you love. You often get what you give.

More specifically on loving behaviour, the words 'I love you' can be easy to say, but it's your body language, how much eye contact you give, your tone and demeanour that can all help to communicate whether or not you are **really** in love with someone. If you love them, maybe put down your phone, stop what you're doing where practicable, keep calm, look at the person like you love them, soften your expression and attitude and give them your full attention with your body. Really try to attune, engage and connect with them. You might even tell yourself in your head that you love this person you're looking at, as a way of ensuring your voice, body and behaviour will be in line with this belief.

Behaviourally, connected love will also be shown in the things you **don't do**. Try not to assume you know what the other person is thinking or going to say. Listen to what they're saying **like it was the first time you've met them**. And if a loved one, or anyone, comes to you with a problem, keep in mind that you don't have to solve it for them. It's okay not to know the answer. Most often, it's enough just to validate ('I can see you're upset') and empathise ('and I understand why'). People most often just want to be seen and heard, rather than being told what to do, because it's the former that they'll frequently have missed out on in a childhood dominated by threat/reward.

In your interactions with others, you now need to notice which part of you you're in and try to use your language **consciously** to manage the direction the interaction is taking. Are you operating in balanced connection or threat when you speak? Is it characterised by connected gratitude, forgiveness, care, patience, support and love, or is there a river of anger, fear, impatience and jealousy running through it? You may have had to be quiet and contain your fear and anger as a child, but is it best serving you now to spend too much of the time saying every threat thing that comes into your mind, when you could be connecting with others?

Of course, the range of your thoughts and feelings should be expressed with other people to encourage intimacy in relationships and this includes threat ones. It's connecting to soothe others and to be soothed. Again, though, it's about balance. Try to be aware that, without management, threat will take a lot of the space between you and others, with its arousing worries, comparisons and complaints. Threat feelings, as you know, are infectious. Be careful not to ramp each other up in a threat/reward-biased echo chamber.

You need to be conscious of your impact on others and know that you can often choose that impact. Keep an eye on humour here in the form of 'teasing' and 'banter'. As you know, humour feels good and can connect. But, we also use humour when we're dictated by threat: 'many a true word said in jest' and 'playing the fool to get away with murder'. Sarcasm is often really just passive aggression and some 'banter' can just be downright aggressive. You're not in the playground or your childhood front room anymore – you don't need to do this or consent to it. Perhaps try to replace a third of the times you tease someone with a compliment or expression of gratitude instead and see how much more connected you feel.

Bear in mind generally that people will associate the adjectives you use to describe others with **your** personality, something identified as 'spontaneous trait transference' in a 1998 Study by Skowronski JJ. et al. If you describe someone else as kind and genuine, people will associate those qualities with you. The reverse is also true – call someone a bitch and people will associate that word with you. Another reason not to be consistently critical of other people. So take responsibility for what you say in conversations and actively manage the verbal pathways you go down to make sure they're mainly about connection. Even get familiar with a few practical, gentle ways to change the course of conversations: 'Did you watch *Game of Thrones* by the way?'

Overall, in terms of the capacity for kindness in people generally, with the news story of the pensioner who was punched to the ground and had his wallet stolen, you know dominant threat biases will preoccupy about the attacker. To move into more balanced connection with others, try to draw your attention also to the passer-by who stopped to hold his hand, the one who called the ambulance, the person who took that call, the paramedics in the ambulance, the nurses and the doctors who treated him, his family and friends who rushed to the hospital, the occupational therapists and physiotherapist he saw afterwards, the victim support volunteer he talked to three days later, the neighbour who does his shopping for him while he recovers and the mates who buy him a drink when he finally gets back to the pub. Think about all these people too, mainly because **that's who you, and most of the people you know, would probably be**.

Give other people the opportunity to mean something different to you now and vice versa. If you avoid others because you believe people are somehow unsafe, you lose the potential to experience the joy of them. And they miss out on the joy of you too, which is a shame, even though you may not quite believe that yet. Always try to keep yourself open – with just a little helpful threat for protection and some helpful reward for fun – and know that, fundamentally, all of us just want to love and be loved and we can all heal each other in trying our best to achieve this.

In terms of helpful threat and self-care, it's also important to think about when to move people out of your life. I've left this until now, because, as you know, threat may be **too good** at cutting people out, except maybe for unconscious caregivers like romantic partners and parents. I often see people tolerate partners and parents who seem to treat them badly as a pattern of behaviour, but cut a 'friend' out of their life because they cancel a drink one night or simply say the 'wrong' thing. This seems to me because too much threat is rooted in a place where you believe you can't survive without your caregiver (and vice versa) and that most friends and acquaintances don't as deeply touch the early caregiving part of us that our partners and parents do.

Whatever the reason you might stay in a toxic relationship – be it fear, love, status reward or a mixture of them – excessive threat/reward can run really deep in other people without any willingness to change on their part. In balanced connection, you don't just forever offer the other cheek if you're treated badly as a pattern of behaviour. You don't need to spend the rest of this life with someone on your metaphorical knees, wondering what on earth you did wrong this time. Some people are just better left untrusted. As much as you'll work to keep connected with people generally, know that you are deserving of love and respect and there is no person in this world you can't live without – there are over 66 million other people in this country alone. At some point you may need to give a person the nod and move on, either reducing contact with them or moving them out of your life completely. And then try to no longer pay them any mind, as you focus on growing other connected relationships. It will be much easier both to do this, and to know who it should be, when you have a loving relationship with yourself.

Having said this, it's a good idea to try to forgive others where necessary too. You know by now that people behave 'badly' largely for the same reasons you do. The main reason you need to try to forgive them is to free yourself from their dominant threat/reward state of mind. The person you're letting off the hook with forgiveness is therefore you. When you hold a grudge, the other person possibly has no idea you're doing it and is probably just getting on with their life. As Malachy McCourt once said: 'resentment is like taking poison and waiting for the other person to die'. So, try to forgive to let go of your hope for a better past – please try to let go of the impossible.

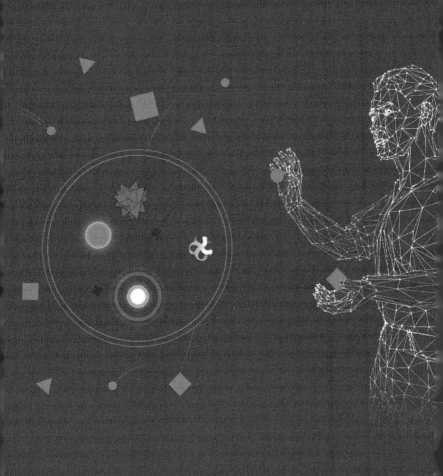

9 choose your
BOUNDARIES

CHAPTER 14

Principle 9: Choose Your Boundaries

Fundamental to you keeping in balanced connection is being aware of, and asserting, healthy boundaries internally and externally.

Internally, boundaries are the behavioural lines you draw for yourself to make sure you're acting in your long-term best interests. They're like the brakes on a bike that, maybe counterintuitively, actually mean you can **enjoy the ride** of your life by feeling safe. Externally, boundaries are the invisible lines drawn at the point where you end and the other person begins – your guidelines on how it's okay for others to behave towards you, how you'll react if they cross them and vice versa.

Healthy boundaries, and your ability to act in line with them, opening and closing them as you need to, are key. Boundaries come from your beliefs, values, moral compass, social environment, opinions and growing up. Based on what you already know, you can probably assume that excessive threat/reward can often have messy, inconsistent and unhelpful boundaries as holding boundaries can conflict with threat/reward survival/reward messages.

Because of your possible lack of connection with feeling, too much threat/reward compromise your awareness of what's okay and what's not for you. You might either struggle to express boundaries or overreact when you put them in. Your walls might be either too tall or collapsed, and you can flip between the two. For reward, very few boundaries are sacred in the pursuit of reward. You can see unhealthy boundaries in some specific threat/reward conditions: in co-dependency – not being clear where you begin and the other person ends – and in addiction – crossing your moral compass over and again to deaden cravings/feel alive.

If you are controlled by threat/reward you might have a tendency to expect others to be very boundaried, while you can act in the unboundaried way that threat/reward justifies. It's the place of enjoying the rights of living as part of a societal system, but being less keen on the obligations: outraged that someone would speak on their mobile phone while driving, as you break the speed limit because you can.

You need to try to make a conscious and ongoing inventory of how boundaries currently manifest, or don't, in your relationships with yourself and others. These can include:

- keeping time
- honouring commitments
- having a clear idea of what rewarding/fun/pleasurable/ entertaining behaviour is okay for you and what isn't
- when to take a risk
- saying no if you don't want to do something
- saying yes if you do want to do something
- if and when to challenge feedback
- making it clear that you're okay/not okay with a behaviour
- disagreeing/agreeing with others
- listening to and not interrupting others
- keeping promises to yourself and others
- whether you get enough privacy
- whether you're living with integrity
- whose ideas you take on board and when
- keeping confidences
- when to reach out for help and support and when to try to sort it out on your own
- when to offer help and opinions to others and make suggestions
- whether to accept something if you don't agree with it
- how you use humour (accepting that in your own head, you decide what's funny; in relationships with another, they do)
- containing your threat thoughts before you say them
- what's your business and what isn't
- when to work through conflict in relationships

- when to stand apart from a group if you're uncomfortable with what's happening
- how you manage money
- your morals
- the difference between care and support of another and rescuing/pathological caretaking
- how porous you are to messages from others about who you are
- the kind of questions you ask, and the subjects you raise, when socialising
- physical/touch boundaries
- the extent to which you're psychologically 'enmeshed' with another. Is there anyone's approval/disapproval you care more about than a grown adult really should?

Once you notice your boundaries, or lack of, you can begin to bring them more into accordance with balanced connection. You need to have firm boundaries to keep you safe **and** also be able to reach out to others as you need to. As ever, it's **balance** you're looking for here and it's a journey, sometimes of trial and error. Some boundaries may need to be strengthened, others lessened. Initially, just be curious about where these lines in the sand are.

A way to hold boundaries is by keeping your nervous system in a balanced state, to maintain your ability to breathe, reflect and hold a nice, wide view of yourself and the world. And there's no rush – if you fear voicing unhappiness with others, it may be enough initially for you just to be aware you're unhappy with them and spend time imagining how you might say this in a calm and balanced way. It may be some way down the line before you can override threat enough to **say** it and that's okay.

You might also **imagine** what a boundary looks like between you and others. You need boundaries that are permeable enough to allow flow and flexibility in interactions with other people, but consistent and firm enough for the incoming to bounce off where needed and for you to keep your grounded sense of who you are as you relate to them. The idea of 'winding up the window' can be helpful here. You can see, hear and relate to the other person from the other side of the window, but there's something clear in between you both that acknowledges and maintains your separateness.

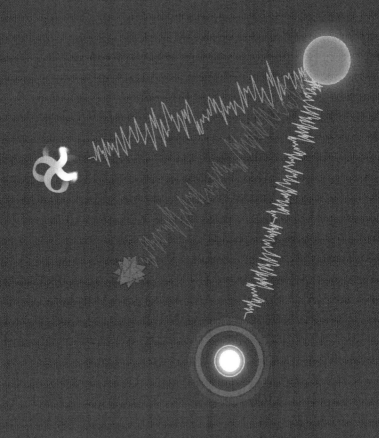

10 Focus on COMMUNICATION

CHAPTER 15

Principle 10: Focus on Communication

Most of this chapter is really about communicating distress, but, just to make the point, one of the most important things you can now use communication for is to connect with other people: try to tell them you love them, thank them, praise them, compliment them, support them, validate them and empathise with them, as often as you can.

In terms of distress, when threat/reward are too dominant you may have a preference for talking **about** and not **to**, because:

- of your frequent outward-in focus

- you believe direct communication of your unhappiness could be confrontational

- you're often not really sure what to say in a balanced connection way that's easier for the person to hear

- of a lack of trust in the other person to respond well

- you might struggle to self-soothe/regulate/control your own threat if you do get into 'the talk'

You might shy away from direct, open communication, unless you're angry, and you're going to be far from open and empathetic when you're angry. You might also show your anger in passive aggression, silence and oppositional behaviour, none of which get your needs met. You might believe that to express certain feelings is 'weak' or means you're 'vulnerable', such as tears, fear, love and/or gratitude. Your nervous system might also become so aroused that your clear thinking, and therefore communication, is compromised. If you are dictated by reward, you may have secrets and lies, which restrict open, honest and helpful communication. Helpful words can therefore hide from you, so you now really need to try to find them as a way to connect with yourself and others and to hold boundaries.

Moving to balanced connection therefore involves consciously reflecting on how you communicate. Try to hold in mind that clear, balanced communication is the way you get many of your emotional needs met in relationships with yourself and others. Notice when you're talking about others behind their back rather than to them and ask whether this is helpful. Talking to friends about another friend, for example, can be a good way to work through what you think and feel about them and even put unhelpful threat concerns into perspective, but you also know that, if complaining about your friend or your partner is all you do as a pattern of behaviour, it'll just feed resentment and reinforce unhelpful threat/reward.

In a situation in which you're unhappy, try to think about what you don't like, why this is the case and what you're going to do about it. As you know, you then have three choices: you accept it (which means no longer complaining about it); you change it (possibly by suggesting changes to the other person, but most often by changing how you are with them); or you leave the relationship. All are possible balanced connection options, but try to do one of them sooner rather than later and to know why.

Before you say something, perhaps think about whether, in the grand scheme of things, this is worth doing. As you now know, just because you're frightened or angry about something, doesn't mean you should be. You know your threat biases will often heighten the importance of any potential problems, sensitise you to them, you may even imagine them. Try therefore to test threat with a balanced nervous system before saying anything, rather than having a policy of 'speaking your mind'. Think in terms of choosing whether or not to **respond**, rather than threat **reacting**, when you're unhappy about something. Wherever possible, don't allow threat to be in charge when you speak to others and choose **the right time** – when both of your nervous systems are balanced, therefore receptive and therefore capable of empathy and connection. This way, you can be sure you say what you mean, that you mean what you say and that, to the extent you're in control of this, the other person will be doing the same.

More specifically, when you choose to express something, try to:

- Calmly plan what you're going to say.

- Stick to the matter in hand and the facts, notwithstanding that the latter will be subjective. Don't maraud around in the past with lists of wrongs and resentments – try to keep to the now.

- Speak gently, evenly and with empathy, as far as possible. If threat starts to turn your volume up, the other person's threat will naturally start to raise their voice too.

- Own what you're saying. Threat often uses 'you' and the permanent/pervasive references to 'always' and 'never'. Try to use 'I' when you speak and be balanced, nuanced and expansive when explaining what's happening for you.

- Explain what you're feeling bearing in mind that nobody can 'make' you feel anything. You know that underneath your anger is always likely to be hurt, a sense of unfairness or fear. I'd tend to describe them more. To put this into words, you might therefore say, 'When [x] happens, I feel [y] and [z] is what I'd like you to do differently.'

- Leave it to the other person once you've made it clear how you'd like something to change. Try not to engage in threat's short-term need to dominate, control and win. Relationships are a process of growth, change and possible rupture and repair over time, so avoid fights to the death. Trust that, because the other loves/likes you, your message will percolate through to a change, or at least result in a good reason why that's proving difficult. It's then up to you whether you accept any lack of change in due course, or leave the relationship.

- Bring any discussion to an end when you notice either of you is experiencing threat too intensely. You know the biases and distortions of threat, so try to realise you're going to struggle to engage in helpful, productive dialogue when in it. If you're both angry, both of you believe you're a victim of the other and both of you believe you're hard done by, the discussion is unlikely to make progress.

An interesting point to remember here is that you could actually see assertiveness as being **in control of yourself**, of threat, rather than any ability to control others. If **you** try to remain calm, you preserve access to your memory, reasoned thinking, perspective and empathy. The other person will also often mirror this behaviour without thinking about it. You'll therefore be much more likely to get your message across and, in turn, be heard by the other person and therefore both get your needs met.

Some people spend so long having to be quiet during a dominant threat childhood and adolescence, that they tend to want to scream all their adult life. This isn't helpful either. I'd suggest you do your best to never respond in anger to any situation in your life unless it's a real threat. Always give yourself at least, say, four hours to calm down before responding if you're angry about something. Your anger may just hear someone else's reasons for what they've done, or not done, as excuses and **only** see your point of view. You want your guide to be **speaking for, advocating for**, threat, rather than **speaking from** it. If you get angry, try to draw it to a close with a commitment to come back to it at another time. Relationships are a long game. You can go back and talk about something any time you choose. And it's really important that you do go back. If each time you do you move to threat, maybe think about some relationship counselling.

Do also try to apologise when you need to. And for every time you raise an issue, bear in mind you need to have spent more time communicating your gratitude to the other person and the things you like about them, just to keep **balance** in the face of both your biases. Crudely, it's the 'shit sandwich', but we're not talking about making things up to soften the blow, just to hold an expansive, and therefore more accurate, view of the other person than threat allows you.

Conclusion

To be human can mean the greatest and the worst. In any one moment, you can be the venom or the antidote. And that's okay, because you now know **you decide which it's going to be**.

Try to take full responsibility for the fact that your quality of life depends on your choice in any one moment between your parts. You know that the ultimate control and power to strive for now, is this control and power over yourself.

You can choose to leave fake news dominant threat/reward in charge and give death and/or relentless reward the greatest power over your life, continuing in their trance. Bouncing up and down between these two, dulling your shine and pulled in the wrong directions. Doing enough just to get by, often frightened of shadows. Mostly avoiding, wandering and wanting, just enduring.

Or, you can decide enough is enough now, choose to be defined by problems in your past no longer, to stop making somethings out of nothings and, instead, engage in self-directed neuroplasticity. To break the spell, get out of your own way and remedy your brain's inbuilt design flaws standing in between you and more sustained contentment, satisfaction and well-being. Deliberately and intentionally managing your attention, your biases and your nervous system. Stacking your deck more in your favour now. Making doors you can walk through where there used to be walls. Optimising your huge potential for creativity, peace and happiness.

Try to hold in mind that you now need to stop internal fighting. Turn in to the world behind your eyes with curiosity. Exploring relationships internally and externally. Patiently and gently assessing all that makes up you and your life. Noticing the extent to which your experience has been, and carries on being, tainted by unhelpful threat/reward. You'll hold onto and value what's great and good enough and let go of the threat/reward aspects that no longer serve you, building balanced connection alternatives.

To do this, the 10 principles mostly manage your attention to focus on connection. As threat and reward were born with the biggest muscles, you're now building your connection ones. Doing so of itself crowds out unhelpful threat/reward. Rather than ruminate over your 'mistakes', you'll try to manage your attention to the good things that you've done and do more of them. You skip more often to the good stuff, plant your own seeds and focus on your own life, gradually moving to balance your parts in the process. **A balance of both being and becoming. Of calmness and aliveness. Of effort and ease.**

Whether it's through your thoughts, feelings, behaviours and/or body, you know you can work bottom up or top down; outward-in or inward-out… breathe, relax, sing, say no to something you don't want to go to, say yes to something you do, sit very still, drink more water, be grateful, learn something new, stop, smile, contact an old friend, cultivate plants, open your arms, think how you can improve a current relationship, look at old photos of good times, sleep more, smile again, slow down, go on a rollercoaster, visualise what your heart looks like in your chest for three minutes, wear what you want to, eat slowly, have a sauna, soften your hands, turn your face to the sun, draw, sit by some water, dance, put down the weed, look at the moonlight, turn your phone off more often, write your empathetic life story, take a warm shower, meditate, complain less, listen, go for that promotion, tell others what you like and want, lie down, stand tall, go to a party, run, give way more when driving, cut your nails, stop again, compliment someone, say sorry and mean it, go for a walk, challenge yourself, sunbathe, listen more, make a list of what's great about you, chin up, kiss them like you'll never see them again, make a list of what's great about your partner, smell flowers, slow and deepen your breath, look at the stars, listen to the birds, wait calmly for your turn, rest, smile for no other reason than you're alive, compete in a race, actually taste your food, have a couple of glasses of wine/pints of beer with friends, relax your shoulders and belly, affirm you're safe and loved, tell others you love them, cool down, warm up, think of who inspires you, spend a little less time on social media… the list is endless and different for everyone. As long as you take responsibility and take back your time and life for balanced connection.

Maybe this is widening your window of tolerance, a more waking life, new neural pathways, coming out of your shell, giving your children a childhood they don't have to recover from or finding yourself. Whatever you call it, with a strong guide maintaining a balance of your parts and the dominance of connection, you'll unfold and expand as threat/reward's false barriers fade. Instead of going outwards to fill the internal void they can create, you'll most often be standing, satisfied, on the golden sweet spot of balanced connection.

With balanced connection in place, you'll be better able to catch and hold yourself when threat tips you into threat feelings or reward craves. Actively coping, rather than avoiding and/or attaching. **Anything can happen outside, but not inside anymore.** Threat is recalibrated to your fundamentally safe and potentially loving environment. And reward is managed to ensure that it **doesn't** calibrate to all the opportunities for reward in your environment. Your stars of thinking, feeling, behaviour and body are more aligned to work for your common good. You might realise in the process that you're not actually the centre of the universe. Perhaps not as superior as you needed to believe you were. You'll probably slow down, and almost certainly have more subtle and reflective relationships internally and externally.

With **a balanced connection**, you'll realise you and others are full up with value and worth already. You'll often experience greater impulse control and be as esoteric as you want to be, not because you're scared and angry, but because that's who you are. You'll be healthier and more expressive, your language will evolve, you'll feel more free, content and spontaneous and have happier and more sustainable relationships. You'll build and live a life with more meaning and purpose that you don't need holidays from. Today will look forward to being tomorrow. So this is what it feels like. It's about time right? Enjoy your new-found freedom, my friend. Live your balanced connection life. **Yes you can. You've got this.**

THE BEGINNING